Hotels of the
Old West

Hotels of
the Old West

Richard A. Van Orman

INDIANA UNIVERSITY PRESS

This book is a publication of
Indiana University Press
Office of Scholarly Publishing
Herman B Wells Library 350
1320 East 10th Street
Bloomington, Indiana 47405 USA

iupress.indiana.edu

Manufactured in the United States of America

Original 1966 Edition *A Room for the Night* Library of Congress
Catalog Control Number: 66-22441

ISBN 978-0-253-04270-5 <pbk>

1 2 3 4 5 23 22 21 20 19

To Bonnie

CONTENTS

ILLUSTRATIONS

PREFACE

IN THE ARTICLES, MONOGRAPHS, AND BOOKS DEVOTED TO the trans-Mississippi West, scant attention has been given an important and fascinating institution—the Western hotel. Nineteenth-century travelers and tourists who experienced actual contact have written more on this subject than have professional historians and dedicated buffs. A significant reason for this is that the West is continually depicted in "blood and thunder" terms, and what does not fit easily into the pattern is discarded. In that seared land of Indian fights, badmen, and the Pony Express, hotels are overlooked.

A colorful segment of Western life was acted out in the rooms, bars, and restaurants of these establishments, which varied from grandiose to grimy. The crude structures offered as accommodations to travelers by mining camps and cow towns were uncomfortable, unrestful, crowded and dirty; their proprietors were appropriately rough. With the influx of Eastern and foreign travelers, however, and the resulting demand for adequate and pleasant public accommodation, Western hotels underwent a transformation.

To enthusiastic Westerners, hotels stood for permanency

and prosperity as only a multi-storied, many-roomed structure could. They were an integral part of those days of ambitious schemes and freewheeling optimism; as the poem "The Wheelbarrow Man" avers, "Speculation is the fashion even at this early stage, and corner lots and big hotels appear to be the rage." To sophisticated, critical Europeans and Easterners the incessant hotel building seemed indeed a mania. It appeared to them that Westerners were vying with one another for the opportunity to reside in these public houses, most of which the tourists considered unfit for human habitation. With upturned noses and upset stomachs, these visitors came, coughed dust, and complained.

No matter how much the optimistic Westerner bragged about splendid hotels and lavish banquets, to most of those outsiders the West was still primarily a land of houses "with pompous names and limited accommodations," with flies and bedbugs, quick-tempered landlords, and rude employees.

Such extremes of living were found in few other regions of the world. Juxtaposing the raw with the regal, the Western hotel offers the historian a fertile field for research.

To the following libraries I owe a considerable debt: Indiana University and Lilly libraries, Bloomington; Newberry and Chicago Historical Society libraries, Chicago; New York Public Library, New York City; Bancroft Library at the University of California, Berkeley; Henry E. Huntington Library, San Marino, California; and the Rosenberg Library, Galveston, Texas.

But more important are the librarians who have shown me the way: Eleanor Rogers and Kathryn Troxel at Indiana University; Carolyn Berg, Texas State Historical Association,

Austin; Elizabeth Comfort, State Historical Society of Missouri, Columbia; Elizabeth Stevenson of the Rosenberg Library; and Mary Isabel Fry of the Huntington Library. My appreciation also goes to George Jelinek of Ellsworth, Kansas; Robert E. Eagan of Dodge City, Kansas; and to the late Lucius Beebe of Virginia City, Nevada. To Professor Oscar O. Winther of Indiana University, who has made numerous excellent suggestions and whose idea this subject was, I owe a personal debt. And to my wife and coauthor, Bonnie, I enthusiastically offer my deepest thanks.

RICHARD A. VAN ORMAN

Hotels of the
Old West

[1]

Hospitality of the Old West

IN THE ISOLATED WEST THE FORBIDDING LAND, INCLEMENT weather, and implacable Indians were impediments to the struggle westward. Across this seemingly limitless expanse, the settler in his roles as innkeeper and storekeeper extended hospitality to those unprepared and less fortunate. In a harsh and demanding environment, he was willing to aid and comfort strangers.

A cultured widow from Kentucky, Mrs. Mary Austin Holley (cousin of Stephen F. Austin), visited Texas in 1831 and found in that distant polyglot land that hospitality was the rule, with everything freely offered to a newcomer. Obviously, this early Texas booster concluded, Texans did not have the polish and refinement of Europeans, but their open-handedness was honest and warm. Six years later, a sojourner in the newly-formed Republic of Texas avowed that no other

3

persons observed the forms of hospitality as conscientiously as the older Texans. This anonymous Ohio author praised them for being unselfish in their welcome to a stranger, sharing all they had while receiving nothing in return except "the pleasure which a noble nature always derives from acts of generosity." There were others who would agree with him. In the 1840's a well-to-do German merchant in the Lone Star State was surprised to find that hospitality was the rule and not the exception. And a Texas pioneer remembered that no one ever considered charging a stranger for lodging; in fact, it was deemed an insult to offer to pay for bed and board.[1] Nevertheless, it was usually the wealthier Texans who offered free lodging and food to travelers; frequently the poorer settlers expected a dollar for a meal and a bed.

Though Texans' kindness to strangers was storied about, the zenith of Western hospitality was attained by the California rancheros. Before the Gold Rush and its accompanying migrations those garrulous and carefree Californians, brought up in the Spanish-Mexican tradition of *hospitalidad,* were happy to accommodate passers-by in their unpretentious adobe *casas.* California rancher and politician John Bidwell, in the first immigrant train to reach California in 1841, recalled that their friendliness had not been exaggerated. Meals, entertainment, and beds were free in that courteous "demiparadise," and if a man wanted to travel he was welcome to borrow a horse from adjoining ranchos along the way. Reverend Walter Colton, alcalde of Monterey, commented on the boundless hospitality of the Californians in the late 1840's: "They are always glad to see you, come when you may; take a pleasure in entertaining you while you remain; and only regret that your business calls you away."[2] The height of liberality was attained when "guest silver" was provided for needy visitors. Coins were laid out on a table and covered with a cloth, and it was a point of honor with the ranchero not to count them after a guest departed.

Until secularized, the twenty-one Franciscan missions were as well known for their welcomes as were the ranchos. In that Arcadia a man could journey northward along *El Camino Real* from the mission at San Diego to the one at Sonoma and be charged not one peso for food, bed, bath, and a fresh horse. A historian of the region boasted, not without reason, that Californians were the most gracious hosts in the world.[3]

This early tradition of hospitality no doubt owes something to the loneliness born of isolation and the eager desire to see new faces and hear reports of the outside world. So long as travelers were few, hotels were unnecessary. Yet even after the hordes of gold seekers arrived and hotels sprang up, hospitality did not vanish. A Connecticut-born forty-niner wrote that California miners were the friendliest and most charitable men that ever lived. And the Eastern philanthropist and welfare worker, Charles L. Brace, was pleased to find that liberal welcomes were still evident over a decade later; the first words addressed to him were, "Well, you have come to spend a month, of course."[4]

As generous as California hospitality appears, that of the range was more widely practiced. In a region where distances were measured in bleached bones and unmarked graves, hospitality constituted an unwritten code. England-born cowhand "Teddy Blue" reminisced about his many years on the range: "You had to feed and shelter your worst enemy if he came to your house in a storm, and if you refused him shelter, you had better leave that country." A common greeting was "Jest tie up your hoss in the old corral, en 'light, stranger, 'light!" One cook remembered that his camp always fed and lodged travelers; when they arrived it was " 'Light and fill up," and when they left, "So long, boys; stop again."[5]

Writing two decades after his trail-driving days, one drover swore that his outfit would have been happy to entertain an outlaw or an angel if only the newcomer wouldn't talk about cows.[6] In winter, when work was scarce, a roving wrangler could ride the grub line. Going from one outfit to another, he freely received food, shelter, and a fresh mount in exchange for news and companionship.

The "zest of novelty" that visitors brought guaranteed them an enjoyable stay. Misinformed British travelers expecting less than friendly receptions were surprised at many "cow country" courtesies. In 1877 Arthur P. Vivian, a member of Parliament, on his way to California remarked that Platte Valley ranchers showed a sincere willingness to furnish his party with lodging and meals. Staying at a Wyoming cattle ranch during the winter of 1880-1881, an English hunter was given all that he needed. On many occasions this sportsman stayed two or three days at the ranches, and not a cent was requested when he departed.[7] The unique experience of having a foreign guest was seemingly payment enough for these ranchers, and it was a conversation piece for months afterward.

Like remote ranches, army posts were solitary and drab but welcomed all. Major George A. Forsyth, an able cavalry officer, explained that at these forts "hospitality was a virtue that exercise never tired; it was practised in a way that gave to the wanderers from the haunts of civilization a new meaning to the word." After hunting in the Powder River country in the fall of 1880 a British major found officers at Fort Fetterman, Wyoming Territory, gracious to his party. And, even though their means for entertaining were limited, a similar greeting was offered another Britisher at Fort Riley, Kansas, where the commanding officer promised proper cheer and friendly company.[8]

To many travelers Western hospitality was more unexpected and surprising than an encounter with slovenly Indians, bandy-legged cowboys, or garish prostitutes. Arthur Vivian never ceased to be amazed by courteous treatment, and was startled to find that Westerners "were hospitable and generous to a degree hard to find in more civilized life." In Dakota Territory neighborly wagoners invited the vigorous French nobleman, Edmond Mandat-Grancey, to share their dinner of bacon, beans, and coffee. When the Frenchman proffered two dollars to the headman in payment for the dinner, the latter indignantly refused the money.[9]

But by the 1850's the increasing migrations westward brought about a diminishing of hospitality, and there were some who took unfair advantage of travelers. Charging exorbitant prices, raffish and dishonest sharpers squatted on or near main-traveled trails to prey on optimistic overlanders. In his journey to the Pike's Peak gold fields in 1860, a young fortune hunter encountered at the three-year-old hamlet of Capioma, Kansas Territory, a group of leeches who took all the money they could from distressed travelers. Indeed, the

7

entire way swarmed with swindlers and rogues who were quick to profit from the helplessness of others. Needy, tired travelers were cozened "by as scurvy a set of bipeds as ever demoralized any community." At an isolated Kansas ranch, wretched water was sold for five cents a glass. Whiskey was added in an attempt to conceal its staggering stench. A youth of nineteen, James K. P. Miller, en route to the turbulent placer-mining camp of Virginia City, Montana Territory, was irritated because few of the farmers along the way were either willing or able to offer any food or supplies, other than a cup of water.[10]

As more settlers trudged westward because of the mining rushes, there sprang up on the more frequently traveled stage and wagon routes a frail line of business establishments. Appearing first in the 1850's in Kansas and Nebraska, these noisome, fly-infested stops were called trading posts, stations, or, more often, road ranches. Often located in groves of cottonwood trees along sandy streams, they combined the functions of hotel, bar, restaurant, post office, store, and polling place. The erudite Cincinnati lawyer and banker, James F. Meline, a summer traveler in 1866, pictured a Nebraska road ranch (sometimes spelled "ranche") as "not a dwelling, nor a farm-house, nor a store, nor a tavern, but all of these, and more." A stop 400 miles west of St. Joseph, Missouri, was described by Richard F. Burton, the flamboyant British explorer and scholar who had recently discovered Lake Tanganyika, as resembling a Parsi's shop in western India, equipped with everything from a bottle of champagne to a needle.[11]

If a wayfarer struck one of these traffic stations (and in 1860 there were approximately a hundred between Omaha and Denver), he might find "decidedly Nebraskaish" entertainment and high-priced provisions such as salt, coffee, tobacco, canned meats, fruits, vegetables, butter, eggs, knives, playing cards, and colored goggles. These hostelries also sold a horrible whiskey variously called "forty rod," "tangleleg," and "bust head" which was likely to bring out all the bad habits of the consumer. Often this concoction was made of tobacco, molasses, red peppers, alcohol, and what passed for water and had the potency to "make a humming-bird spit in a rattlesnake's eye!" Upon asking for whiskey, a thirsty traveler in Colorado was told that there would be a short delay, for the watered-down ranch brew had frozen in the jug the previous night and was in the process of thawing.[12]

The selling of road ranch "rotgut" at ten dollars a gallon was a lucrative enterprise at these roadside inns. But it was the sale of fodder and the trading of draft animals, usually oxen, which brought the greatest profits. After miles of torturous travel the hooves of oxen often became too sore for further pulling. A ready rancher was delighted to swap a healthy ox for two sorefooted ones. These jaded animals were then turned out to graze and, if not killed by Indians, would in a short time be fit to retrade or sell for $100 to $130 apiece.[13]

Indian trade was another profitable adjunct to road ranching. In exchange for whiskey, sugar, coffee, mirrors, combs, and various baubles, Indians bartered buffalo robes and tongues, antelope skins, buckskins, and, on occasion, their women. In turn, the ranchers made excellent profits by selling the pelts to travelers and at Missouri River ports. Several ranchmen sent intrepid agents, working on a percentage, to live with the redskins and direct trade to their ranches. J. K. and Jud Gilmans' cedar-built ranch in Nebraska, located close to Indian and white trails near the fork of the Platte, was reported to be worth over $50,000 in 1863.[14]

Generally inhabited by "rude specimens of humanity" dressed Indian fashion in elk and deerskins with matching manners, those adobe, log, or sod houses were filthy and overrun with bedbugs, dogs, and children. In the vernacular of the time it was said that the distance to civilization was measurable by the growth of a rancher's lousy hair and the prices he charged.

Hostile utterances were common among unhappy travelers who believed that isolation and quick returns had warped the ranchers' sense of moral obligation. A disgruntled Pike's Peaker was convinced that one qualification useful in running a ranch was a background in horse stealing. Fitz Hugh Ludlow, a New Yorker traveling to California for his health, complained that many stationkeepers took pleasure in inflicting innumerable discourtesies on travelers; their women were no better, serving miserable meals with "an air of personal insult."[15]

However, had carping customers known the precarious existence of a ranch family, they might have better understood their strange and often crude manners. Sickness, storms, and savages made a rancher's life hazardous. For protection against the Indians, many road ranches were enclosed by palisades. The buildings (ranch house, barn, storehouse) were next to the walls of the palisade with the center used as a corral for the stock. Some ranches had watchtowers, and in times of danger around-the-clock lookouts were posted. But it was the height, usually six feet, and thickness, two to four feet, of the turf or log walls that offered the best protection against Indian attacks.[16]

Several Indian traders such as John Richards and Joe Bissonette held that a more practical and less expensive way to deter Indian depredations was to take a redskin wife. Still, such arrangements did not always benefit the squaw man. "French Pete" (Louis Gasseau) lived in an improvised wooden shack in Dakota Territory with his Sioux wife and their five half-breed children. On a July morning in 1866 he was found mutilated, killed by a party of Sioux.[17]

James Meline was amazed by the risks the road ranchers and their families took. Upon asking a ranchman if he would move his family to safety at signs of an Indian attack, the realistic owner responded "No, . . . where should I go? All I have is here. They burned my house and killed my stock two years ago, and I'll stay and see it out." Another reacted to Meline's persistent concern by asserting that he would "Give 'em the best I've got," nodding toward his rifle. But a woman rancher was unimpressed by talk of Indian raids, and declared she would not be convinced of the danger until she was scalped.[18]

The effect of hostile forays on the determination of the ranchers and settlers was negligible. With the end of the Civil War, traffic west in the spring and summer of the late 1860's was again heavy. One Nebraska road rancher was so inconvenienced by incessant queries that he posted a question and answer sheet. After giving distances between certain points, it continued:[19]

11

Are you a married man?
No sir E.
Don't you want a wife?
Well, wouldn't object.
How long have you lived here?
2 years.
Do you like it?
Well I does.
What's the name of this place?
Fox's Springs.
How old are you?
None of your d—d business,
Have you any pies?
Yes Sir.
How do you sell whisky?
15 cents a drink.

The largest and most famous of the Western stations was Jack A. Morrow's cedar-built Junction Ranch in Nebraska at the junction of the North Platte and South Platte, 360 miles west of booming Atchison, Kansas. Before Morrow opened his ranch in 1860, he had worked as a teamster and had been a partner in a trading post. Some swore that the sociable but "dangerous-looking" Morrow was in league with a band of cutthroats who supposedly rustled overlanders' stock. But he seemed to have had a way with the ladies, for a colonel's wife was satisfied that he was "the prince of ranchmen, and the king of good fellows," while a captain's wife judged him a considerate and convivial gentleman.[20] Perhaps they had never learned of Morrow's Indian wife, his wild poker games, or his drinking bouts, which were storied from Denver to

Omaha. Because some travelers avoided his ranch, Morrow dug a deep ditch, forcing them to a route which passed his stop. A few years later, when the Union Pacific Railroad by-passed his ranch, Morrow ferried his three-story building over to the northern bank of the South Platte and for a time thrived next to the tracks. He later moved to Omaha, where he engaged in land speculation, and died penniless in 1885.

Road ranchers, like hotelmen, came from many walks of life—farmers, freighters, fur trappers, miners, soldiers—and, again like hotelmen, they strongly believed in the value of advertising. In the manner of hotels which advertised comfortable beds, cheap rates, and fine meals, a Platte Valley rancher boasted "a large and secure 'Correll' in which the stock put in our care will be put every night. Terms $1 a Head per night." A few years before the Arapaho and Cheyenne burned down the American Ranch, "a Home for the Weary" in Colorado, the owners announced in the *Huntsman's Echo,* one of the first newspapers published west of the Missouri River, that they had on hand fodder, food, whiskey, tobacco, and anything else a traveler might require.[21] Gifted with a rare sense of hyperbole, Samuel Hyde advertised his ranch in large type in the Kearney *Herald,* a weekly newspaper that contained many Nebraska road ranch notices:[22]

> Be pleased to give us a call, and taste of the viands, smell of a smile, and loose your animals to the forage, and if you don't go away feeling better, your stock moving livelier, and your whole outfit looking refreshed, then say Sam. Hyde isn't a good ranche-man. Don't forget the place—Valley Ranche, situated in the very heart of that Canaan-like valley, the charming Platte.

At times travelers were forced to stay overnight in a ranch's pilgrim quarters because of bad weather, signs of Indians, or sickness; slumber, however, was rarely peaceful. A soldier's wife spent sleepless nights at two stops. The first was in Nevada, where she stayed in an apartment with fifteen men. At the second, in Arizona, she shared a bed with another woman and worried "whether or not I, who occupied the side next the wall, should be shoved through it." In 1875 at a ranch in the Southwest, the sleep of an army wife was interrupted by wildcats jumping into her room through an uncovered window. Her husband threw his boots at the intruders but the cats returned, pursued by barking mongrels.[23]

Graphically describing the nature of the land and its inhabitants, "Dirty Woman's," "Pretty Woman's," and "Fort Wicked" were some of the road ranch names. "Fort Wicked" in eastern Colorado was so named because its bearded owner, Hollen Godfrey, and his wife killed seventeen Indians during a two-day attack in January, 1865. The appellation "Dirty Woman's," also in Colorado, was chosen because the proprietress supposedly "died of dirt." The liberal Pennsylvania editor, Alexander K. McClure, and his wife Matilda stayed at that one-story, four room hovel where the flyspecked walls were decorated, incongruously, with *Harper's Weekly* and the *Atlantic Monthly*. Mrs. McClure considered that the readable wallpaper was utilitarian as well as decorative. A lieutenant's wife from Indiana found the name "Dirty Woman's" fitting. Upon entering, she spied the proprietress with broom in hand hitting a pig which had caught its neck in the cream jar. After much striking, swearing, and squealing, jar and pig rolled into the yard. Richard Burton described one ranch as being as "civilized" as an African hut. A canvas partition divided the hovel in half, and dogs and logs covered the earthen floor. Posts served as chairs, planks were made into tables, gravel was used as soap, and evaporation took the place of towels.[24]

While not devoted entirely to trade, stage stations, like road ranches, were placed at ten- to thirty-mile intervals and offered shelter as well as foul sleeping accommodations, wretched food, high-priced provender, and slimy liquor. Spotting an adobe station with a grass roof, Sam Clemens, traveling to Nevada in 1861, remarked that it was the first time he had ever seen a front yard on top of a house. Clemens noticed the limited washing facilities at the station and described a comb that could have been handed down from Samson and Esau, gathering hair ever since—as well as "certain impurities." Similar conditions were noted by a French mineralogist journeying by stage to Colorado in 1867. At stations along the way combs, brushes, mirrors, and even toothbrushes were fastened together on long strings for public use.[25]

The prairie monitor, or dugout, which served as protection against Indian attacks, was a unique type of stage station, built underground and connected to the stables by a subterranean passage. The most famous was Dugway, a hundred miles west of Salt Lake City. There, as at most stations, passengers could buy for one dollar coffee with no sugar or milk, rough bread, and malodorous bacon. Between Atchison and Denver, stage passengers ate the meat of the region, buffalo and antelope steaks. Stops in southern Nebraska and northern Kansas offered chicken, cream, butter, eggs, and vegetables.

In 1863 near Atchison the cost of a meal was fifty cents; as the stage clattered farther west the price rose to seventy-five cents; and between Julesburg and Denver it jumped to two dollars.

Those who had been warned about stage station food before their journey stuffed bags and pockets with dried beef, cheese and crackers, canned herring, hard-boiled eggs, and bologna. At one filthy stop a flustered passenger complained to the owner about the dirt, whereupon the latter responded, "Well, sir, I was taught long ago that we must all eat a 'peck of dirt'." The guest agreed, "but I don't like to eat mine all at once." Biscuits green with saleratus and meat steeped in fat were some of the repulsive viands served at stage stops. After two days of miserable meals at stations in New Mexico, one traveler was in no mood for a Negro attendant who appeared at the coach door and intoned, "Say, you fell's! want any breakfast heah?" The disgusted passenger kicked the greeter and told him to go to hell! William H. Dixon, an English magazine editor never noted for his tact, put it succinctly: "The food is bad, the water worse, the cooking worst."[26]

Three years after that statement was made, an event took place that would spell the end to stage stations and road ranches. With the driving of the Golden Spike on that cold, clear May Monday in 1869 at Promontory Point, Utah, began the incredible Western railroad era. The celebration was showy and loud. With amazed Paiutes looking on, champagne was tippled, guns were fired, and a marvelous future was predicted for the West. For the road ranchers, however, the next few years were dark and declining. Soon the long, snake-like procession of wagon trains would halt, the sale of whiskey would end, and the demand for goggles would not be heard again until the appearance of the automobile. A few determined road ranchers who lived near the tracks turned their stations into train stops; some became cattle ranchers; but most closed their doors and drifted away to find other employment.

Road ranches had served their purpose. They provided what the emigrants needed, and had saved some travelers from death. Moreover, these ranches showed that cattle could survive and even fatten on the native, dried grasses of the open plains, a fact that would be of utmost importance to the coming cattlemen.

Living beyond the fringes of settlement, the Western inhabitants reflected in their primitive speech, dress, and manners what it was like to be a pioneer. They lived with reckless courage, and displayed to outsiders an apparent disregard for the safety and health of their families. In their desperate discomfort and desolation they survived for twenty years and, when they left, never again did such men appear in the West.

[2]

Early Western Hotels

SETTLERS MOVED INTO THE NEWLY-FOUNDED TEXAS REPUBLIC
in the late 1830's, attracted by the lure of cheap land. Galveston, Houston, Austin, and San Antonio, the four principal
towns, euphemistically labeled certain abodes "hotels." Ten
years later, public houses appeared in Independence, Westport,
and St. Joseph, Missouri, where pioneers, nervous with ex-
pectation of the May journey overland, came in sufficient
numbers to increase a landlord's likelihood of an early retire-
ment. Hotel profits were also sizable in Lawrence, Atchison,
and Leavenworth, despite strife in Kansas created by the in-
tense sectional feelings in the decade before the Civil War.
And although San Francisco made an inauspicious start,
grand hotel life flowed into that boisterous Bay City with the
bullion from the California and Nevada mines.

Texas houses, like most early Western hotels, not only supplied beds, meals, and liquor but provided places to hold
meetings, religious services, cotillions, concerts, trials, wed-

18

dings, and funerals. And where there were no hospitals, the sick were brought to hotels. Though these houses were often filled, complaints were frequent about poor victuals, dirt, vermin, distant outhouses, repulsive odors, and sharing beds. In many hotels there was no such thing as a private bed. Sometimes two or more men slept together. In a few cases, the sexes were mixed in the same bed. Even chickens, dogs, and cats might share a bed with a sleeping guest. Rates were high and the furnishings of the rudest sort with mattresses of Spanish moss, corn husks, and prairie grass. One unhappy wayfarer, upon receiving his bill from a Texas landlord, responded, "If you come to insult me again sir, by [God] I'll shoot you sir."[1] Recognizing the potential hazards in such a business, the proprietor of Houston's Fannin House charged two dollars a day for board, but demanded ten dollars from intoxicated guests.

In 1840 Galveston had 3,000 inhabitants, a few sorry wooden hovels, streets littered with decaying oysters, and the Tremont House. When nearing completion in the fall of 1837, this house was blown down by a hurricane. Finally opened in April, 1839, the three-story structure, advertised as among the "best Hotels in the United States," became famous for its lavish banquets and balls.[2]

British diplomat Francis C. Sheridan, grandson of the Irish dramatist Richard Brinsley Sheridan, visited the Tremont ten months after it opened and made note of Texas' peculiar hotel procedures. At eight in the morning the guests were awakened by some "fiend" ringing a bell. A few minutes later a second ringing, announcing breakfast, brought a flurry of guests streaming into the dining room; ten minutes later they bolted out. Dinner was conducted in the same frenzied manner. After a hurried supper the stuffed boarders, with nothing to do, whittled, drank, and smoked cigars until bedtime.

In his cramped bedroom, Sheridan noticed a stove before which some roomers were taking a "quiet spit." That night he awoke from a fretful dream to find the room stifling, and was bothered by a dissonant duet between the stove and his snoring companions. The next morning Sheridan's ablutions were brief, for a cracked mirror in the bathroom caused him to nearly shave off his nose. Seeking a safer shave at a barber shop, he entered one which displayed color prints of Napoleon and Andrew Jackson under which hung the notice "Gentlemen That Washes In This Shop & Does Not Get Barbered At The Time Must Pay 12½ Cents To The Shop."[3]

Fifty miles from Galveston, Houston in 1837 was all noise and construction. One of the buildings going up was that town's first hotel, a "spacious wooden shack," the City. Another early hotel, the two-story Mansion, was operated from 1837 to 1840 by Mrs. Pamelia Mann, one of the town's most colorful citizens, who was once sentenced to hang. That unruly vixen in April, 1836, loaned a team of draft oxen to General Sam Houston a few days before the Battle of San Jacinto. When Houston decided to attack General Santa Anna's Mexican troops, she demanded the return of her team and, after waving a pistol, she got them. Six years later Sam Houston, then President of the Texas Republic, had difficulties with another Texas landlady. Deciding that Washington-on-the-Brazos, where Texas independence was declared, would make a better capital than Austin, Houston dispatched an army officer to Austin to secretly remove the government archives. While loading the bulky materials into his wagon, he was spotted by hotel owner Mrs. Angelina B. Eberly, whose business would have been hurt by Houston's proposed move. The "War of the Archives" began when she rushed over to a six-pound cannon loaded with grape and fired on (but missed) the surprised intruder.[4] The archives were later buried in tin boxes by the citizens of Austin.

Opened in 1840, the rambling Houston House, though losing money, aspired to be the social center of the untamed town. Competition came from the peach-colored Old Capitol Hotel, "situated in the most healthy part of the city," which had served from 1837 to 1839 and again in 1842 as the capitol of the Texas Republic. In the winter of 1844 an English couple, traveling for their health, lodged at the Houston. Leathery beefsteaks and cold eggs were served for breakfast. But they were more shocked, as was Sheridan, at the haste with which the guests ate, none staying at the table more than five minutes.[5]

Sleeping accommodations proved to be a further source of irritation to the fatigued pair. A norther blew coldly through the many crevices in the hotel's wooden walls that night, extinguishing the candle in the couple's bedroom. Overhead a sleepless cat clawed pieces out of the canvas roof, while below the two travelers placed an umbrella over their bed for protection.[6]

Fifteen miles outside Houston on the main road to Austin, a widow advertised her tavern for sale—"commodious dwelling house and all necessary outhouses," along with shade trees and "10 or 12 gentle Cows"—a picture of bucolic bliss, but the reality was something else. Touring Texas back-country in the 1850's, Frederick Law Olmsted, journalist and critic of the antebellum South, noted that most public houses in Texas were nothing more than log cabins with crowded, dirty rooms and poor food. At one, breakfast was "a succession of burnt flesh of swine and bulls, decaying vegetables, and sour and mouldy farinaceous glues, all pervaded with rancid butter." In another, Olmsted was surprised to see one of his sleeping companions "gravely *spit*" out the candle before hopping into bed, explaining "it gave him time to see what was about before it went out."[7]

An international incident was created at Austin's two-year-old Bullock House in 1841 when the first French minister to Texas, Alphonse de Saligny, refused to pay his bill on the ground that the rates were too high. The envoy left the hotel and moved into a private dwelling next door. A short time later, a few of Richard Bullock's hogs ate some of the Frenchman's provender. In return, de Saligny's servant killed twenty of the pigs, whereupon the irate Bullock thrashed the servant. The "pig incident" became a diplomatic incident when, in part because of it, a $5,000,000 loan from a French banking house to the Republic of Texas was canceled.[8]

After Texas became a state and had no need for foreign aid or haughty French diplomats, there opened in San Antonio the then finest hotel in Texas—the fifty-room, two-story Menger. Migrating from Germany to the United States, William A. Menger, a cooper by trade, opened a brewery in San Antonio in 1855. With money made from his excellent beer and with a wife experienced in running a rooming house, Menger built his hotel. It was opened on February 1, 1859, with an inspection by the townspeople, and the highlight of the evening was free lager beer. Years later, a woman magazine writer from Massachusetts described her entrance into the house, down a stone passageway and out on a wide courtyard "surrounded on three sides by open galleries, with the stars overhead, and the lamp-light flaring on a big mulberry-tree. . . . You feel that you are in the heart of Old Spain."[9] Night masked the spots and cracks of many hotels, but it brought beauty to the Menger.

Famous for parties, its bar, and cuisine, especially the turtle soup, the Menger was later to become known for its visiting celebrities—Generals Phil Sheridan and U. S. Grant, Sidney Lanier, William Sydney Porter (O. Henry), and Theodore Roosevelt, who recruited some of his famous Rough Riders in the Menger bar.

Richard King of the King Ranch was a frequent guest at the Menger. (In fact he eventually died there and his funeral was held in the hotel.) During one sojourn, the hot-tempered King grew impatient waiting for water to be brought to his suite. Waiting no longer, he went to the second-floor railing and dropped a water pitcher to the marbled lobby floor, yelling, "If we can't get any water up here, we don't need a pitcher." Water was quickly drawn for the angry Texan. At a Galveston hotel, after quaffing his favorite drink, Rose Bud whiskey, King grumbled to the headwaiter about a tough piece of meat. As nothing was done about the matter, King left his table, ordered a complete meal across the street, and returned with it. Finding his dirty dishes still on the table, King dumped them to the floor.[10]

Although they had few fine hotels, Texans gave them high-sounding names—Grand Windsor, Mansion, Tremont. With the exception of St. Louis, Missouri hotels were of no better quality, nor were their names so grand as those of the Texas hotels. Buzzard's Roost, Arrow Rock, and Cross Keys were some of the Missouri houses, and their atmospheres usually matched their names. At these crude establishments business was discussed, religion preached, politics debated, and courts convened. A bed to oneself cost twenty-five cents, with two in it twelve and a half cents. One tavern, Montbrun's, was located in a cave on the Missouri River. Another, in Danville, was run by a preacher and afforded him a wonderful opportunity both to comfort and save his guests. Major Isaac Van Bibber managed a popular tavern in conjunction with a dancing school at Loutre Lick, but the old man was considered odd by his roomers because he often expounded abstruse ideas. On one occasion this eccentric friend of Daniel Boone mentioned to three Kentuckians his theory that all events recur every 6,000 years. After pondering this statement, his lodgers informed Van Bibber that they would pay their bills the next time they happened by in a few thousand years.[11]

Farther from the main routes of travel, however, other accommodations for travelers were more like homes than inns. Here it often became a ticklish matter whether a guest should pay. Not wishing to offend by offering money, many travelers presented payment to the youngest child and then noted the parents' reactions. If the uncertain sojourner detected unhappy expressions, he would quickly take back the money from the confused child. Confusion was not limited to children. At a Missouri lodginghouse run by a widow, a traveler was perplexed by a four-poster. Never having seen

24

MENGER HOTEL, SAN ANTONIO

ATCHISON, TOPEKA AND SANTA FE DEPOT, TOPEKA, KANSAS, 1880

(Santa Fe Railway)

one before, he could not imagine how to get in it. He climbed on a table and leaped over the top, but instead of landing on the feathers, he went through to the floor.[12]

Missouri's hotel era began with James W. Marshall's discovery of gold in California. With the opening of the Western floodgates, the outfitting towns along the Missouri River soon had hotels for those who were tired of sleeping under the stars or in crowded Conestoga wagons. Business was seasonal but profits were large. In the spring the Harris in Westport, the Merchants of Independence, and the Pacific and Patee houses in St. Joseph were visited by westward migrants. Even though the floors were uncertain, the blankets unclean, and the price $2.50 a day, most wayfarers were thankful that beds were available.

Until surpassed in the 1870's by San Francisco, St. Louis had the best hotels in the West. As gold and silver had helped build the former's hotels, the fur trade had built the early hostelries of St. Louis. The two-story, stone Missouri, opened in 1819, was then its most prominent house. A year later, in the dining room, the first state legislature met and elected Missouri's first United States Senators, David Barton and Thomas Hart Benton. Benton's victory has been attributed to the fact that the legislators met in a hotel, for Representative Daniel Ralls, a Benton supporter near death, was carried in his bed from his upstairs room to cast his vote for Benton.[13]

Many Western communities devoted their initial years to trade, mining, or cattle, and were not concerned with good hotels. But as time passed and money was available for investment, thoughts turned to building up the towns and making them more respectable. Thus began the age of the Western hotel. To optimistic townspeople a hotel, like the railroad, promised to create population and wealth. And the larger the hotel, the greater the future of the town. The hotel filled the need for a business establishment, lured travelers and tourists, and was therefore an important symbol to the Westerner. The bigger the dream, the taller and finer the hotel, and vice versa. Where hotels were concerned, the practical Westerner contained a bit of the dewy-eyed visionary.

So it was in St. Louis. Thanks to local capital, long-term credit, and ready citizens, there came the larger, grander hotels—the National, the City, and the Planters'. Construction on this second Planters', the first having opened in 1817, was started in 1837 after some of the city's influential citizens, looking to the future of St. Louis, decided to build a grand hotel. In the building of these city houses one committee selected the site, another was set up to obtain stock subscriptions. Then a board of directors was elected and a charter drawn up. Many hotels, however, were built before there was need for them. Unfortunately, these frenetic investments often led, especially in smaller communities, to a string of bankrupt hotels and towns; instead of bringing stability, they brought insolvency.

On April 1, 1841, the Planters', soon to be famous for its "assemblies" and its wealthy Southern guests, was opened by former lessees of the National with the customary dinner-dance. One year later English novelist Charles Dickens noted that while the hotel was excellent and provided many "creature comforts," it was constructed "like an English hospital, with long passages and bare walls, and skylights above the room—doors for the free circulation of air."[14] With exceptional longevity for a hotel, it closed in 1890; former United States Senator David H. Armstrong, who had lived there for years, refused to move: "I'll be damned if I'll evacuate the quarters which have been my home for so many years, and if they want to put me out they will have to eject me by law."

By the close of the Civil War, four of the more than fifty St. Louis hotels were the six-story Barnum, the Pacific, the Southern, and that "enormous pile," the 530-room Lindell, completed in 1863 and, at that time, the largest hotel in the United States. But the most prominent was the Southern, which had taken eight years to finish. Planning began in 1857 when a few St. Louis citizens determined that the city again needed a new hotel. The usual boisterous meetings were held; architects' drawings were submitted; a hotel company was formed; and a state charter was obtained. But because of economic dislocations the initial enthusiasm languished, and the project was put aside. Three years later, however, the state legislature granted the company a ten-year exemption from county and city property taxes. With this financial impetus, construction began and continued through the Civil War, and on December 6, 1865, the six-story Southern was opened with a magnificent ball. For the next twelve years it was the city's best hotel. In the early morning of April 10, 1877, however, a fire broke out in the basement and, because of the lack of sufficient hose pressure to reach the upper floors, the Southern was destroyed with a loss of thirteen lives. One of the many guests to escape was newspaperman Joseph Pulitzer. Another Southern, supposedly fireproof, was completed in 1881 and included 350 rooms, steam heat, and five hydraulic elevators or "vertical rooms."[15]

In 1854, while St. Louis was witnessing an expansion in hotel construction, Lawrence, Kansas, was being founded by the antislavery New England Emigrant Aid Company, which had been organized to settle Kansas with people devoted to the "love of freedom." The company was inundating the recently-formed territory with free-state settlers and needed headquarters, so it purchased for its colonizing members and other free-soilers Kansas City's Gillis Hotel, which was soon called the Free State.

Proslavery Missourians settled Lecompton, Leavenworth, and Atchison, and organized "Blue Lodges" to protect the slave interests and to chase out the free-soilers. By 1856 Kansas towns and their citizens were violently split by the passions of the sectional controversy. That year Leavenworth's three-story, brick Planters' was finished. Although it accommodated guests of free-state sentiment, most were of Southern persuasion and, to placate its customers, the management had on duty at all times one proslavery and one free-state bartender.

Tensions increased and in late April, 1856, a pro-slavery sheriff was shot and critically wounded in Lawrence. In retaliation Lawrence was pillaged on May 21 by 800 proslavery "border ruffians." The two newspaper offices were destroyed; and Shalor W. Eldridge, lessee of the newly-built Free State, was given two hours to remove the hotel's furnishings. Because this house was the property of the Emigrant Aid Company, it was especially hated by the Southerners. When the

29

time was up, a Mexican War cannon was fired on the hotel, but did little damage to the stone and concrete. Finally, the Free State was put to the torch.[16] Reopened in December, 1858, it was again burned down on a hot August day in 1863 by William Clarke Quantrill's plundering guerrillas after they had robbed the guests. In other regions of the West there were also hotels which were known as Southern or Northern houses, depending upon the sentiments of landlords, employees, or guests. (The United States in Los Angeles was closed in 1861 by Captain Winfield Scott Hancock because it was "notorious for sedition.") But in no other area was violence directed at hotels.

Violence was rare in tranquil California when its first public house, Vioget's, opened in 1840 in Yerba Buena (renamed San Francisco in 1847). Six years later two sailors from the United States sloop of war *Portsmouth* built a sign for the hotel and its name was changed to Portsmouth. During the same year Brown's, later the City, was given its finishing touches and, until the Gold Rush, this one-story adobe was San Francisco's best hotel. Shortly after it opened, the City was almost destroyed when the crew of the *Vandelia,* celebrating the Fourth of July, fired several cannon salutes, the last one hitting the house.[17]

In the late 1840's and early 1850's, with the influx of frantic fortune seekers who had neither the time nor the inclination to build houses, numerous hotels sprang up in San Francisco. Because of the shoddy construction of these and other buildings, the town had six major fires between Christmas, 1849, and the summer of 1851. To many people, progress was connected with fires, for after each conflagration a better city would be built. Hotels were built, burned down, and rebuilt with monotonous regularity. Most of these were two-story shanties, or *gîte* houses, constructed of rough boards and covered with canvas in which one room served as office, bar, bedroom, and kitchen. Tables were made of boxes, chairs were fashioned out of barrels, and on the floors were lumpy mattresses stuffed with straw and broken crockery. Sheets were uncommon, but not dirty pillows, foul blankets, and nocturnal visitations "by the third plague of Egypt, accompanied by a liliputian host of the flea tribe." With whiskey providing more warmth than the bedding, a boarder might find a few hours of rest. Sleeping places were chalked out on the floor when all the mattresses were in use.

Like ships, these hotels were fitted with rows of numbered bunk beds which were simply four-tier-high canvas or rough boards extending to the ceiling. This was a dangerous arrangement, for men on the lower cots faced the probability of being stepped on, kicked in the head, or, more commonly, spat upon.

San Francisco's Montgomery House was described by Sarah Royce, mother of the philosopher and teacher Josiah Royce, as being covered outside with canvas, boards, and sheets of zinc, with the inside cloth-lined. Upon entering the carpetless parlor, she noted that it was separated from the dining room by a cloth partition. The bar was larger than the sitting room and had the only stove. On the second floor, she walked down the narrow hall to her two-and-a-half by six-foot room with bunk beds; and as no other accommodations were available, she was grateful for these.[18]

Housing a hundred persons in a room and charging each a dollar a night, landlords found it more profitable to work the miners than to work the mines. In 1849 a bed in a room with fifty bunks cost six dollars a week. At the St. Francis, which had the finest sleeping rooms in town, board and room was $150 per month.[19] Other early San Francisco hotels were the Delmonico, Astor, Revere, United States, and America. Because the best-known hotel names were in use, late-arriving landlords were at a loss to find appropriate appellations for their houses.

With building costs high and materials limited, deserted ships were converted into saloons and jails, and the *Niantic* became the Ship Hotel in 1851. Because of such expenses, the Graham House was packed in parts in Baltimore and shipped around the Horn to San Francisco. If building materials were scarce, money was no object. In the Union Hotel a cigar stand rented for $4,000 a month. The El Dorado, a blue gambling tent, rented for $40,000 yearly. The two-story wooden Parker House, which burned down three times, had as many billiard and gambling tables as beds. For $10,000 a month that hotel rented out its lower floor to gamblers, and nightly could be heard a cacophony of striking billiard balls, popping corks, jangling coins, tinkling glasses, and the blare of a bugle.[20] The miners had little to do with their gold except gamble it away; hence monte, roulette, and faro brought in more revenue than room and board combined.

One of the most unusual hotels in the West was the What Cheer House, named for a then common English salutation, whose guests were primarily miners, farmers, and mechanics. Built in 1852, the What Cheer was a man's refuge from trouble—women were forbidden to enter. Fifty cents in advance was the price for a room with a clean bed, clear water, towel, and a piece of soap. On arriving, a roomer bought tickets at fifty cents apiece to pay for his meals and room; he was reimbursed if he left before using all of the coupons. Over 4,000 meals were served daily, including 1,200 eggs, 100 pounds of butter, 500 pounds of potatoes, and 400 quarts of milk. Reminders such as "Butter free, with two ten-cent dishes," and "No bread with one fish-ball," were placed on the menu for the benefit of the guests. Surprisingly, for it had a rough clientele, the What Cheer was a temperance house.[21]

The What Cheer was known for its exotic rooms—a bootblacking room where a guest could clean his own shoes, a fine museum filled with 600 stuffed birds, pickled reptiles, coins, shells, and Indian curios. In its well-patronized 3,000-volume library, free to all guests, rugged-looking miners read studies on beekeeping and stock raising, newspapers from the East and Europe, *Harper's* and the *Overland Monthly,* and novels by Dickens, Cooper, and Scott. Landlord R. B. Woodward's yearly bill for the library was over $1,000, but his profits were close to $50,000.[22]

South of San Francisco was the slowly-growing pueblo of Los Angeles and its famous Bella Union. When youthful Horace Bell saw that two-story hotel in 1852, three years after it was opened, he described it as a "flat-roofed adobe," with "pigeon-holes, or dog-kennels" for rooms. If a guest was respectable, he might be granted the privilege of sleeping on a billiard table, which often made the best bed, unless a drunk in the night decided to shoot a game. The Bella

Union's unsmiling bartender had a double-barreled shotgun and three Colt revolvers nearby, for the customers were the "most bandit, cut-throat looking set" that Bell had ever encountered.[23]

In 1858 a doctor, about to embark on a military expedition against the Mojave Indians, hoped for a good night's rest in the Bella Union, but the commotion was unrelenting. A guest staggered down the hall and into bed and soon began snorting like a pig. The aroused guests threw sticks, bootjacks, and shoes at his door. Still he snorted. Finally they went back to bed, frustrated by his "unresisting apathy."[24] In most Western hotels a waiter rang a bell to notify guests that meals were served, but the management of the Bella Union placed a steam whistle on the roof and its shrill blast hastened the diners to the tables.

One day in 1866 gunshots stirred the guests. A quarrel ended in a gun battle with two killed and one seriously wounded. In the melee a bystander was shot in the thigh, ten others had their clothes perforated with wild shots, and a stage horse in front of the hotel was hit.[25]

Other Los Angeles hotels were the Nadeau, Lafayette, United States, and the eighty-room Pico, a three-story house opened in 1870 boasting gas lighting throughout and a parrot that spoke Spanish.

Lacking the genteel atmosphere which pervaded many of the Eastern hotels, the early Western hotel, like the land, was a man's world, rough in furnishings, raw in features. The West had more hotels and fewer comforts than any place else in the world.

[3]

Mining Camp and Cow Town Hotels

NO HOUSES TYPIFIED THE MALE INFLUENCE OR THE BOOM-and-bust extremes of Western life as much as mining camp hotels. These flimsy structures, the products of fast, often sloppy construction programs, reflected the temporary nature of mining town booms. One-story and filthy, they contained plenty of bar accommodation but only one or two large bedrooms filled with tiers of wooden bunks, pillows made of hay, never-washed blankets, spotted and broken mirrors, brown soap in sardine cans, and water barrels crawling with "wiggle-tails"—all for one dollar a night. Noise and spitting, especially at stoves, were common features, as were arguments between guests who wanted the doors and windows open and those who didn't.

During the Gold Rush, Louise A. K. S. Clappe, known as "Dame Shirley," asserted that California in 1851 could be named "the Hotel State, so completely is she inundated with taverns, boarding-houses, etc." This doctor's wife, from Massachusetts probably noticed that many buildings called hotels or houses were not only for board and lodging but also gambling and harlotry. She stopped at the Empire Hotel in Rich Bar on Feather River, formerly a brothel, when this "impertinent apology" for a hotel was the only two-story building in town. Rough planks and a canvas roof were some of its features and, on the front, large letters advertised "The Empire."[1]

"Dame Shirley" entered a spacious apartment, part of which served as a shop where leather, velveteen, calico, and flannel shirts were displayed next to oysters, preserved meats, ham, and other foods. The rest was the bar, where hung "that eternal crimson calico, which flushes the whole social life of the 'Golden State,' with its everlasting red," remnants of the former fun-loving occupants. In the middle of the calico was a handsome mirror embellished by decanters, vessels of brandied fruit, "forming a *tout ensemble* of dazzling splendor." Benches, a green-clothed table with a monte deck, a backgammon board, and a heap of "yellow kivered" books filled what space was left. Up four steps was the parlor, with straw carpet, mirror, a fourteen-foot-long "aching back" sofa, six chairs, a cooking stove, and red calico curtains. Four steps up from the parlor and she was on the second floor, where on either side of the narrow entry were four bedrooms. These cubicles had frail doors hung on leather hinges, oilcloth tables, and heavy bedstands which looked as if they had been built piece by piece on the spot.[2]

Besides the mining camp hotels, California had teamster

hotels, mainly in the Sierra Nevada Mountains near the Nevada border. Freighting bullion from the Nevada mines to Sacramento, the boisterous and bawdy teamsters were well treated at these small houses and often were given free drinks and cigars, for if one of them did not like a house, all would give the place the "go-by."

Nevada's Comstock Lode became that territory's first great mining discovery after miners learned that the "blue stuff" was silver. In 1865 J. Ross Browne, the ubiquitous Dublin-born reporter, lodged at the best hotel in that "mud-hole," Virginia City. Browne's room was directly over the kitchen, and the heat became unbearable. Not wishing to be "lodged and baked," he vacated the house, abandoned his two-dollar advance, and went to another hotel, which was little better, for the partitions were so thin that he was aware of every happening in the hotel.[3]

Crowding was the rule in Nevada hotels; Browne witnessed 300 men sleeping in "a tinder-box not bigger than a first-class hen-coop!" He told of rooms so scarce in the new state capital of Carson City during a senatorial contest that one newspaper claimed it would cost $10.00 a night to sleep in an old sugar barrel; $7.50 for the use of a crockery crate filled with straw, $5.75 without straw; and $3.50 for roosting on a pole. John W. Clampitt, who traveled extensively in the West in 1867, observed that all the ground in Virginia City was covered with shacks which passed themselves off as boardinghouses and hotels. At some, the small rooms were crammed with men every night. Three hundred miners were piled from attic to ground at the Hotel de Haystack, lying "like winnows in the fields of sickled grain."[4]

Hotel accommodations in Virginia City were less crowded. The three-story International Hotel, erected in 1860, cost $14,000 exclusive of furniture. Most of the furnishings had been borne to town in mule-drawn wagons over the Sierras. Hotelmen seldom missed a chance for quick profits; when there was a silver strike in the Reese River region in 1862, part of the house was taken down, loaded on wagons, and hauled eastward to the new town, Austin.

Another International was soon built in Virginia City and for over ten years it was the social center of the state. After the second one burned down, the third and largest International was opened in 1876, and became the stopping place for celebrities and the bonanza kings who made the hotel their home while inspecting the diggings. Special guests were allowed in the cavernous wine cellar, where they could help themselves. The house was a landmark in the slowly dying town until it burned down in the winter of 1914.

Three years after Nevada's first rush, Montana's mining age began with gold discoveries on Grasshopper Creek in 1862. A year later, Montana's Virgina City was laid out on Alder Gulch, and hotel owners discovered another lucrative territory. By 1864 the town had eight hotels. James Miller, a guest at the jerry-built Missouri House, spent $14.00 a week for board and lodging complete with leaky roof.[5] Albert D. Richardson, the famed Civil War correspondent for the New York *Tribune,* applied to a Virginia City hotel the same criticism expressed by a wayfarer in Illinois who had been promised the room that Senator Stephen A. Douglas had just vacated. When the guest entered the apartment, seven men were sleeping in four beds. He explained to the landlord that, although it was an honor to sleep in a room so recently occupied by the great Douglas, "I *will not* sleep with the whole democratic party!"⁶

Helena, in Last Chance Gulch, was settled in 1864 and offered travelers the International, "one of the best conducted hotels in the mountains"; the Walla Walla, "having a corps of polite and obliging waiters, with some of the best cooks of the United States"; and the St. Louis, which "never . . . had a bill disputed." But such advertising notwithstanding, when a woman at a Helena hotel naively expected privacy and asked for her doorkey, she was given her first tenderfoot laugh by the tough clientele, who were required to leave their guns in the safe.⁷

Montana's copper boom in the 1880's helped build a $300,000 hotel at Anaconda. The Montana was owned by Ireland-born Marcus Daly, one of the owners of the Anaconda mine. As it neared completion one of Daly's partners, tall and bushy-bearded George Hearst, inspecting the unfinished structure, observed, "Better give it another coat. It looks squatty." When it officially opened on July 1, 1889, the four-story Montana included among its furnishings Oriental rugs, a grand piano, pier-glass mirrors, paintings of frolicking nudes, glistening chandeliers, and a mahogany bar. In the floor of the barroom was inlaid a $3,000 wood mosaic of the head of Daly's favorite race horse, Tammany, and anyone caught standing on it was forced to buy drinks for everyone in the room. The ludicrousness of building large houses in underpopulated Western areas was clearly shown when Daly was often the only guest at the Montana; but to maintain appearances he kept a full staff on at all times.⁸

39

The cycle of overbuilding was repeated in Colorado. In 1859 rumors of gold discoveries spread, and the "Pike's Peak Rush" was on. Towns appeared and landlords threw up hotels, some charging five dollars a night for a bed and two dollars for the privilege of sleeping in a chair. But as time passed, respectability became as important as riches, and several fine houses were built. One of them was the Teller House in Central City, which an Ohio journalist thought would be "creditable" even in the Buckeye State.[9]

Civic pride built more Western hotels than any hardheaded business sense, and there was usually more talk than money. Such was the case of the Teller until railroad president Henry M. Teller (later United States Senator and Secretary of the Interior) came to the financial rescue and offered $20,000 if Central City would furnish the hotel site. Public subscription secured the land and unadulterated optimism caught up with Teller, who raised his offer to $60,000. In June, 1872, when the brick hotel opened, it had cost $87,000 and was the largest (with four stories) and best hotel in Colorado. Thirty-one-year-old William H. Bush, former mathematics teacher from Kalamazoo, Michigan, and sometime hotelman from Kansas, was hired as manager. A year after it was completed President Ulysses S. Grant visited the hotel. In honor of the occasion the sidewalk in front was temporarily paved with $1,300 worth of silver bricks and, as Grant walked across them, a few overzealous boys in the crowd tried to knock off his top hat with snowballs.[10]

The Teller and the approach of the Colorado Central Railroad from nearby Black Hawk brought to the community visions of a glorious future in which Central City would become a great industrial city, surpassing Denver with busy factories, palatial homes, and towering hotels. An expression of Mark Twain's aply fits this type of town promotion: "They danced blithely out to enjoy a rainbow, and got struck by lightning."

In lawless Leadville, miners were happy to pay for the opportunity to sleep on sawdust floors in smoky saloons, suddenly to be awakened by a burst of profanity or the gunshots of drunken miners. Others slept in dry goods boxes on sidewalks or crawled into piles of hay in alleys. Some were found dead in the morning from exposure. Leadville, it was said, boasted one of the fastest-growing cemeteries in Colorado. When the weather turned cold, canvas and cloth tents were erected; wagons and caves provided makeshift shelters.

A youthful magazine reporter noted in 1879 that large tents, one recently used at the Philadelphia Centennial Exhibition, were thrown up in Leadville. Mattress factories sprang up and blankets were prized possessions. One of these entrepreneurs had formerly run a wholesale grocery business in New York City. Failing in that, he entered Leadville broke and quickly noticed the lack of housing. Borrowing funds, he erected a huge "shed of slabs" and crammed it with bunks two tiers high to accommodate 500 roomers a night. Here the sheets were clean, the mattresses soft, the blankets heavy, and cracks between the boards allowed for ample ventilation. The proprietor did a great business at fifty cents a night. His rules were stringent, considering the disposition of his clientele—"No talking or laughing, or singing, or drinking."[11]

MINING TOWN

(from John W. Clampitt, *Echoes from the Rocky Mountains*)

In 1879 the three-story frame Clarendon was erected in Leadville. For the gastronomically minded, the hotel chef, Monsieur L. Lapierce, was brought from Delmonico's in New York. Advertised as the "Headquarters for Miners and Capitalists," its owner was the same William Bush who had been the successful manager of the Teller. Upon leaving that hotel, he moved to Leadville and was fortunate in his speculations. Having decided to build the hotel, Bush suffered delays similar to those of others who were forced to bring

42

most of their lumber and materials from Denver. Unforeseen costs and lack of trained workmen slowed construction on the 150-room house, but the work was eventually completed. Another Leadville house was more fortunate financially. With Silver King H. A. W. Tabor subscribing $50,000 to finish construction, this four-story brick structure, opened in July, 1885, was named the Tabor Grand.[12]

In 1879 there was a rush to Teller City, Colorado, followed by the usual hurried pace of town building. To the accompanying thuds of the stamp mills, hotels were built literally overnight. The proprietor of one house then being built told a guest that all finished rooms were taken but that the builders would have a room enclosed for him by nightfall. He took it, delighted with the fact that this was the first time a room had been built around him.[13]

Perhaps the most unusual mining town hostelry was the elegant two-story Hotel de Paris in Georgetown, Colorado. No Western hotel proprietor ever equaled Adolphe François Gerard in taste or temperament. Better known in the community as Louis Dupuy, he was born in France in 1844 and by 1869 had deserted both the French and the United States armies. After coming to Georgetown, Dupuy was hurt in a mine explosion in 1873. A collection was taken up for the injured foreigner and, with this and money earned in a bakery, he erected the Hotel de Paris.

The atmosphere of a small French hostel prevailed in the hotel, whose stucco walls were three feet thick. A statue of Justice adorned the roof and colorful paintings of French and American flags decorated the west side of the house. The ten bedrooms on the second floor were furnished with running water, electricity, Wilton carpets, walnut bedstands, chests of drawers, curtains, and small radiators. The first floor contained reading and sample rooms, kitchen, dining room, and library. The latter included books such as *Les Confessions* by Jean Jacques Rousseau, *Histoire de France* by François Guizot, and *Un Vie d'Artiste* by Alexandre Dumas. With trout taken from a nearby pond, Dupuy prepared an excellent cuisine and served it in the mirrored dining room, where he presided as maître d'hotel. No finer wines than those in his cellar were found in the West; Dupuy claimed that a sip of his wine would conjure up images of sensuous slave girls.

A true gourmet, the little Frenchman also considered himself to be a philosopher, poet, atheist, hater of woman, and lover of beauty; he was credited by Doctor James E. Russell, dean of Teachers' College, Columbia University, as being the stepfather of domestic science in America. Dupuy lived in feudal splendor, refusing to pay taxes; and he was selective in whom he allowed to stay at his house. Dupuy was looked upon as peculiar even after he died in 1900, but he gave the West one of its best small hotels.[14]

The hospitality of the Southwest mining towns was usually adequate for the small number of travelers before the 1880's. An editor wrote that in the area "A stranger, be he poor or princely, is master of the house to which he shall come." But in 1864 Ross Browne, visiting Tucson, could not find lodginghouse, hotel, nor hospitality, and so he slept on the cold mud floor of an outhouse. Browne related the story of a Tucson blacksmith named Burke who invited a friend to stay with him. After spending a bibulous evening, Burke announced it was time to turn in. Arriving with his friend at the town plaza, the host began to disrobe in the street and remarked to his amazed companion, "This is where I gen'-rally sleep."[15]

By 1870 Tucson had a population of 3,224, but Lieutenant John G. Bourke, aide to General George Crook, perceived that it still "enjoyed the singular felicity of not possessing anything in the shape of a hotel."[16] Those who could not gain entry into private homes were forced to bed on ground soft with manure in some fly-infested corral.

Even with the appearance of hotels, public accommodations were not much improved. In 1880 a soldier stayed at Tucson's Cosmopolitan, where office and bar were in the same large room, the only chamber with a wooden floor. Rough-looking men were drinking whiskey and mescal. His small bedroom was filled with a dozen canvas cots, a two-foot space between each. Many of the guests were drunk and a few got into the wrong beds, causing considerable cursing. The germ-infested washroom was equipped with a ten-foot-long wooden sink, seven tin basins, and a barrel of water; the waste water drained into the street. Coarse towels, the usual cracked mirror, and a filthy hairbrush and comb made up the remaining items. This one-story adobe typified Southwestern hotels, offering little ventilation, but many flies and bedbugs, or, as cowboys sang,[17]

> Sure it's one cent for coffee and two cents for bread,
> Three for a steak and five for a bed,
> Sea breeze from the gutter wafts a salt water smell,
> To the festive cowboy in the Southwestern hotel.

"LODGINGS 4 BITS IN ADVANCE"

(from J. Ross Browne, *Adventures in the Apache Country*, Lilly Library, Indiana University)

Like mining town hotels, cow town houses ran the gamut from Western lawlessness to Eastern respectability. After the Civil War, cattle towns boomed for a few hectic, delirious years and then settled down into dull, peaceful hamlets. These communities were railheads between the great herds of Texas cattle and the Eastern markets, and the flotsam of the Western waves descended on them—cowboys, merchants, bankers, gamblers, prostitutes, gunmen, and the ubiquitous hotelkeepers.

The first Kansas cow town was biblically named Abilene. From there an Illinois cattleman, Joseph G. McCoy, had decided that it would be convenient and profitable to ship longhorns on the Kansas Pacific Railroad to the East. When McCoy first arrived in 1867, Abilene was an insignificant dot on the map, had a dozen dirt-roofed cabins and the six-room Bratton Hotel. Nearby, Josiah Jones sold prairie dogs for pets to passing travelers; and before the cattle drives his was one of the hamlet's most lucrative enterprises.[18]

The area was practically unsettled and well watered, with enough grass for McCoy's purposes. Wasting no time, he brought in skilled labor to construct corrals to hold the cattle, a livery stable for horses, and a hotel for the cattlemen—the three-story, frame Drover's Cottage. This $15,000 hotel had forty-five rooms, with plastered walls and green Venetian blinds, a saloon, and billiard parlor, and measured forty by sixty feet. Often seen relaxing on its long porch were the "Drover's Cottage Lords"—cattle buyers, commission agents, and Texas ranchers—exuding a confidence born of the ability to turn a four-dollar cow into a forty-dollar profit.

With the Drover's increasing business, McCoy traveled in the spring of 1868 to St. Louis to find a better manager. He persuaded James W. Gore, steward of the St. Nicholas Hotel, to manage the Drover's. Gore's Samaritan-minded wife Lou, though loud and gruff, soon won the affection and friendship of the Texas cowboys with her motherly understanding and kindness. Mrs. Gore was always prepared to take care of their needs, whether they were tired, broke, or ill. In 1870 Gore purchased the hotel only to sell it that same year. The new owner recognized that Abilene's glory was past in 1872, and hauled parts of his hotel on flatcars to Ellsworth, fifty-nine miles west of Abilene on the Kansas Pacific line.

Ellsworth was founded in 1867 by that railroad; a few months later the Smoky Hill River flooded and swept most of the town away. A new site was selected and showed signs of permanence when a different kind of flood hit—cattle. Ellsworth's first important year was 1871 when 50,000 cattle filled its stockyards and, within two years, they held over 200,000 head. As in other cow towns, every third building was a combination saloon, dance hall, and gambling den, with a special brothel quarter called Nauchville. Among the hotels in Ellsworth—City, American House—the most prominent was the Grand Central, less grand than central. In front of this red brick hotel was a twelve-foot-wide limestone sidewalk, the town's pride and joy. Arthur Larkin, the proprietor, had arrived in Ellsworth in 1867 and built the first hotel, the Larkin. In 1872 he opened the Grand Central, where cavorted such notorious characters as "Buffalo Bill" Cody, "Wild Bill" Hickock, Wyatt Earp, and the infamous Ben and Billy Thompson.[19]

Wichita became a cattle town in 1872, and its hotels— Occidental, Empire, and Metropolitan—were soon crowded with brawling cowboys. A German immigrant built the three-story, $25,000 Douglas Avenue Hotel in 1873, and diagonally across the street was the Texas House; bootblack and dishwasher was Edward L. Doheny, who later became an oil magnate and played a leading role in the Teapot Dome scandal of the 1920's.[20]

When the Atchison, Topeka and Santa Fe construction gangs reached Dodge City in 1872, life began in the last of the important Kansas cow towns. Almost as famous as the Long Branch Saloon, Front Street, and Boot Hill in that

HOTEL DE PARIS DINING ROOM, GEORGETOWN, COLORADO

(Library, State Historical Society of Colorado, Denver)

DODGE HOUSE, DODGE CITY, KANSAS, 1879

(The Kansas State Historical Society, Topeka)

"Beautiful Bibulous Babylon of the Frontier" was the Dodge City Hotel or Dodge House. Opened in 1873 by the firm of Cox and Boyd, it had fifty rooms, served good food and imported wines. A few months after it opened the first shooting occurred when a cowboy attempted to bring a "soiled dove" into the bar. The bartender forbade her to enter and guns were drawn. When the smoke cleared, the cowpuncher was dead and the bartender lay dying.

The famed consumptive dentist John H. "Doc" Holliday carried on a practice in the Dodge House. He advertised in the Dodge City *Times* in 1878, "Where satisfaction is not given money will be refunded."[21]

The sportive sign posted in the lobby of the Dodge House read "Sheets will be changed . . . once in six months—oftener if necessary. When you return, if not able to remove your boots, take off your spurs, it's hard on the sheets. Beds, with or without bugs."[22]

A practical joke was played on a young dude at the Dodge House. The youth was a determined drinker and had been warned that he would start seeing things if his tippling continued. The next time the boy got drunk some of his friends rented an Italian organ-grinder's monkey. When the victim had passed out, he was carried to his room and put to bed; a pistol was placed under his pillow, and the monkey was released in the room. In the morning the young man awoke, spotted the primate at the foot of his bed, leveled the gun and quavered, "Pardner, if you are an imaginary monkey . . . if I am only 'seeing things,' then, O God, I am in a terrible fix, but if you are a real sure enough monkey, then you are in a hell of a fix." He pulled the trigger and the monkey toppled over dead.[23]

Another ludicrous incident occurred when the pet black bear belonging to James H. "Dog" Kelley, saloonkeeper and Dodge City's first mayor, lumbered into a drunken salesman's room and crawled under his bed. In the morning the bear growled and rattled his chain. Upon seeing the beast, the salesman gave a horrible yell, ran out of the room in his night clothes, and dashed into the crowded dining room. He bumped into and fell over a shocked waitress, and both tumbled to the floor. In the confusion, the diners scattered, while the bear wandered outside, where it was soon captured. The story gained in the retelling each day thereafter.[24]

Western life was generally wild and unpredictable and Western hotels were apt to be full of adventure. This was especially true of houses catering to optimistic miners and devil-may-care cowboys. The sights, sounds, and smells of these hotels could turn the stomach of a proper English lady and induce an excitable Eastern traveler to scribble an irritated letter home. But they were simply reflections of Western growing pains.

[4]

Shacks and Palaces

THE MOST WRETCHED CONDITIONS WERE USUALLY FOUND in hotels in areas farthest from the railroads. A horrifying experience befell Lemuel H. Wells, an Episcopal missionary in the Northwest. Upon entering a hotel, Wells was told by the landlord that all beds were taken but one, which would be available after supper. Finishing his meal, he went up to the room and found the sheets soiled and the bed warm. The next morning at breakfast, observing that the other guests shied away from him, Wells asked a fellow diner why everyone treated him so strangely. "Why, you slept in the bed that they took the small pox patient out of last night." Fortunately, the minister had been vaccinated. At another house all the beds were taken, so Wells bedded down by the barroom stove. While he was asleep, a hunter entered with two hounds who snuggled close to the clergyman for warmth. In the morning Wells scratched fleas until he was able to bathe and change clothes.[1]

An abominable hotel in Idaho Territory was situated in a cluster of twenty hovels named Soda Springs where an American ship captain reported that he had seen many dirty holes in his wanderings, but that "shebang," kept by a Mormon, was the "meanest building" he had ever seen. He fared little better at a Keenan City, Idaho, hotel when he slept with another man on a small wooden shelf covered by a horse blanket with his money bag for a pillow. In another Idaho settlement, Silver City, one weary traveler came upon a typical "cloth and paper" hotel, built of boards covered with inexpensive cloth and then papered. The outside was almost as repulsive as the inside. When he lit a candle in his "mere closet, a swarm of big black roaches scampered out from their hundred holes and seemed inclined to dispute possession." The disgusted roomer burned paper to smoke them out, but the smoke bothered him more than it did the bugs. Perhaps the foulest hotel he had ever visited was in Mount Idaho, where, in his "little box" of a room, so much dust arose when his head touched the pillow that it choked him.[2]

Idaho had no monopoly on offensive hotels. In the early 1870's George W. Kennedy, a Methodist minister, experienced similar conditions in Washington Territory. After a tedious ride, his stage stopped in front of a Wallula hotel. When the passengers asked an Irishman in the house if they could get something to eat, he told them that the proprietress had been drunk for two days and meals were not prepared. But curiosity overcame the minister, who peeped into the kitchen. The travelers quickly departed when Kennedy told them that all he had seen was an extremely large hog.[3]

Flimsy partitions did nothing to shut out sound and were

a habitual source of irritation in Western hotels. A Virginia bride who had moved to Montana in 1883 remarked that while staying at a Miles City "tissue-paper" hotel she over-heard some masculine conversations which "both fascinated and embarrassed" her. John Bourke was distracted in a Colorado hotel room by a man and his nightmare on one side of the partition, a mother and child on the other. The child began crying and, to pacify it, the mother babbled on in baby talk. Some of the less considerate roomers yelled at her to "drown him," "stick a clothespin on his nose," "knock the stuffing out of him."[4] A drawback inherent in cloth parti-tions was the fact that often one's outline could be seen by the person in the next room, unless the candle was extin-guished. And if, as happened on occasion, one's foot went through a weak partition on the street side, a strange sight would be afforded passers-by.

Guests were concerned with the lack of privacy in sharing not only a dormitory-like room but a bed, for many Western hotelmen believed there was always room for one more. While in Cheyenne, Foster B. Zincke, an English vicar on vacation, complained about having half a bed, but was told by a young hotel employee that he was foolish to grumble, for the bed was intended to hold three. A well-traveled Englishman visited that town in 1868 and stayed at the Dodge House, which contained only one room for men with twenty-seven beds, one bed for two guests. As for bed com-panions, the Britisher moaned that a tipsy wagoner or worse might flop down and place his loaded pistol under the pillow. Returning to Cheyenne after a three-month absence, this tourist came back to the Dodge House and, not wishing to share a bed again, got one to himself by telling the owner that he had a fever "which though not very dangerous might be troublesome to anyone who caught it." A popular story retold throughout the West centered around an Englishman with the improbable name of Plantagenet Snodgrass who telegraphed a Durango, Colorado, hotel for a private room. The reply came that the hotel had reserved the bridal chamber for him. When he arrived at the house he was shown to his suite—which contained eighteen beds.[5] Snodgrass should have felt fortunate, for he had one of the beds to himself.

While these conditions lasted some years in the West, most travelers soon found better surroundings, especially in the larger towns. San Francisco, Denver, Cheyenne, Salt Lake City, and Omaha, after shaky beginnings, gave to the West its finest houses.

San Francisco was the Western city best known for its hotels. Several factors made the Bay City the hotel capital of the West—its swift growth, its spirit of unbounded optimism, the flood of wealth from the Nevada mines, and a tradition of hotel life. There were few private homes during the town's first flush months, forcing the predominantly male population to lodge at hotels. Its citizens, like many Westerners, believed that a hotel room was the best place to discuss business, give parties, gamble, and enjoy illicit affairs.

San Francisco's first palatial hotel was the three-and-a-half-story Lick House. Opened in 1862 and built in the English Roman style, it became the family hotel of San Francisco. Paintings of buxom nudes, so popular in the mining days, were displaced by tranquil California mountain scenes.

This house, with its marble floors, expensive woodwork, and magnificent dining room, introduced the bridal suite to San Francisco. An eccentric philanthropist, James Lick, was the owner. Born in Pennsylvania in 1796, Lick had worked in Baltimore as a piano maker and had then moved to South America to live for seventeen years. Soon after his arrival in San Francisco in 1847, he made millions in real estate. Lick

"ALWAYS ROOM FOR ONE MORE"

(from J. Ross Browne, *Crusoe's Island*, Lilly Library)

lived out his years at the hotel and became more interested in giving away his fortune—donating $700,000 to the Lick Observatory—than in overseeing his house. Other hotels followed almost yearly, each with its special clientele or "set": the Occidental, the Cosmopolitan, and the Russ. The former, opened in 1863, was popular with Eastern tourists and known for its mineral museum; the Cosmopolitan was favored by Nevada speculators and United States army and navy personnel; the Russ was named for its first owner, Saxony-born Adolph G. Russ, and with its homey atmosphere catered primarily to transients and ranchers. In those "champagne days" between 1860 and 1870, San Francisco's population tripled, the number of hotels quadrupled, and by 1876 there were over seventy hotels in the town. Each was bigger and better than the last one, until the supreme achievement was built—the Palace.

The owner of this $6,000,000 behemoth was the mercurial William C. Ralston. Born in eastern Ohio in 1826, Ralston had had many jobs before coming to San Francisco in 1854 —working in his father's sawmill, clerking on a Mississippi River steamboat, and serving as a shipping agent in Panama. Once in San Francisco, he directed his energy to banking, and ten years after his arrival the Bank of California opened its doors with Darius O. Mills as president, and Ralston as treasurer. This commercial bank soon became the most important financial institution in the Far West, in spite of Ralston's impetuous and generous habits.[6]

In 1872 Ralston became the bank's president, but even then he was thinking of something more important—his hotel. Ralston was no newcomer to the hotel business. He held a fourth interest in San Francisco's newly-built, 400-room, million-dollar Grand, which catered to wealthy families, Eastern and European visitors, and the nabobs of the Nevada mines. It was in part because of the success of the Grand that Ralston decided to undertake the expensive Palace. In planning the Palace Ralston sent his architect, John P. Gaynor, to study and duplicate the Eastern hotels, for hotelmen had few other models except those in Europe. By early 1873 construction had begun, but the hugeness of the hotel taxed California's resources. Skilled workmen were difficult to find and strikes halted the work. Unable to make a deal in the East for furniture, Ralston set up the West Coast Furniture Company and manufactured his own. With the bank's funds he bought a lock and key factory and a forest from which the oak flooring was to be made.[7]

The Palace, symbol of all that was grand and gaudy, was constructed in the form of a rectangle; its most distinguishing feature was the glass-roofed Palm Court, above which were six tiers of balconies. Phaetons and surreys swept awed guests into the well-lighted Court, where Negro bellboys took their baggage, and the guests walked to the massive marble front desk to sign the register. Years later, when the court was no longer used as an entrance, it was crowded with fountains, statuary, and tropical plants. Besides being "earthquake proof," this Western hotel truly staggered the imagination with its Doric columns, arcades, five hydraulic elevators, 9,000 cuspidors, 437 bathtubs, and 31,000,000 bricks. There were four artesian wells with a total output of 28,000 gallons an hour and, in case of fire, there were seven tanks on the roof holding 130,000 gallons of water. Each of the

755 rooms had an automatic fire alarm and a fireplace, while every second room had a private bath. The Palace introduced the "floor clerk" system: on each of the six floors near the elevators there was a desk with a clerk who gave keys, packages, and letters to returning guests. While the hotel was being built in 1875, a San Francisco reporter humorously estimated[8]

> the ground covered by the Palace Hotel to be eleven hundred and fifty-four square miles, six yards, two inches. . . . The weight of the entire edifice . . . is eighty-six billion nine hundred and forty million, six hundred and four thousand, two hundred and one tons, and eleven pounds. . . . Santa Barbara is concealed by a high hill to the south. Arrangements have just been made, however, to have the hill removed or the town jacked up. . . . There are thirty-four elevators . . . four for passengers, ten for baggage and twenty for mixed drinks. Each elevator contains a piano and a bowling alley. . . .

Hundreds of bay windows created the exterior's white "bird cage" effect. San Francisco's earlier houses had been built in the austere English Roman or Italianate style, but the Palace was fashioned in the San Francisco style—a potpourri of Queen Anne, Eastlake, and Second Empire.[9] The only larger American hotel was the United States Hotel at Saratoga Springs, also opened in 1875.

Warren Leland of the famous Vermont hotel family was manager and lessee for the first three years. His nephews, Lewis and Jerome, had run the Occidental in the city ten years earlier. Among his many innovations in the Palace, Leland introduced Negro hotel employees to San Francisco. At one time 150 Negro waiters and forty Negro maids worked in the hotel. Other employees included thirty bartenders, six watchmen, four room clerks, two bookkeepers, a French chef, five assistant cooks, a confectioner from Milan, a Viennese baker, and "Muffin Tom," an old Negro from New York celebrated for his wonderful corn bread and waffles. Leland's "landlordship" was proven in the excellent hotel food and prompt service, but he made one costly error. For the dining room he ordered egg-shell china which lasted less than a week.[10]

The "noblest hotel of the Western World" officially opened on October 2, 1875, with Leland Stanford as the first guest. Less than two months earlier, after a run on his bank had closed its doors, Ralston mysteriously drowned off North Beach. His able but vain partner, William Sharon, Republican Senator from Nevada, became the hotel's sole owner. Sharon soon recognized that the Palace was "four times too large for its period and place," and was able to obtain a million dollar reduction in the assessment. The dream that Ralston and Sharon had had of a large trade between California and the Orient never bore fruit, while the hoped-for traffic from Europe which was to pass through San Francisco on its way to China was detoured by the success of the Suez Canal. Consequently, many of the rooms were vacant; Sharon therefore attempted to sell the house to the United States government to use as post office or customhouse, but the government refused to buy.[11] Still, numerous travelers stopped in the city; as more comfortable and faster trains cut the 3,500-mile coast-to-coast trip to seven days, approximately 300 hotel guests arrived daily at the twelve leading hotels in 1876.

right, CENTRAL COURT, PAL-
ACE HOTEL, SAN FRANCISCO,
CALIFORNIA; *below,* PALACE
HOTEL, SAN FRANCISCO, CALI-
FORNIA, ABOUT 1885

(Bancroft Library, University of California, Berkeley)

The Palace, like many lesser houses, exploited the names of its distinguished guests. According to boasting managers, Generals Ulysses S. Grant and William T. Sherman, and businessmen Cornelius Vanderbilt and Jay Gould stayed at their hotels even before they were built.

The famous, near famous, and the unknown came, gazed, and commented. Dom Pedro II, the long reigning Emperor of Brazil, was so taken with the hotel that he told San Francisco's mayor that nothing caused him to be so ashamed of his country as the Palace. A Chicago newspaper correspondent remarked that it was a house made up of houses—"a kind of architectural Surinam toad that swallows . . . little toads to keep them out of danger"—and would safely conceal a man in hiding, even if his pursuer resided at the Palace. Rudyard Kipling, on his way from India to England in 1889, called the Palace a "seven-storied warren of humanity." A popular hotel magazine facetiously stated that guests at the Palace did not need to go outside for exercise. "Once around the corridors is equal to a mile, and half an hour on the top floor equivalent to a couple of weeks at a mountain or seaside resort."[12]

To illustrate the hotel's vastness there is a story that Robert U. Johnson, an associate editor of *Century Magazine,* had an appointment in his hotel room with the Scotland-born naturalist, John Muir. When the hour of the meeting came, Johnson heard from the corridor, "Johnson, Johnson! where are you?" Johnson responded and Muir's next words were, "I can't make my way through these confounded artificial cañons."[13]

Next to owning a home on Nob Hill, residence at the Palace became the quintessence of snobbery. Song and dance man Eddie Foy reported there were so many millionaires at the Palace that one couldn't have thrown a rock into its lobby "without hitting at least two or three."[14] Because important persons frequently visited the house, one wag implied that California was run from the garish Palace bar.

If one did not have the money to live there, he could hire a cab, drive into the lush court from the Montgomery Street side, and walk around to be seen. To many, it was a never-to-be-forgotten sight when the balconies were lighted up, a band played Strauss waltzes in the Music Pavilion opposite the main entrance, and beautifully dressed ladies promenaded along the wide corridors.

Two years after the Palace opened, another important San Francisco house was finished—the Baldwin. It was owned by Elias J. "Lucky" Baldwin, who had decided to raise a monument to his name on Market Street, and opened in April, 1877. Born in Ohio in 1828, Baldwin had owned a grocery store in Indiana and later a hotel in Racine, Wisconsin; he left for California in 1853 with four wagons, one full of brandy. This six-story rival to the Palace cost over $3,-500,000, and contained $300,000 worth of furniture. To compete with the Palace, Baldwin paid Tiffany's $25,000 for a clock that became the talk of the town; he bought carpets at $25.00 a yard in Philadelphia, and purchased twelve pianos. A theater, Baldwin's Academy of Music, was located in the hotel. This 400-room house, with its mansard roof, cupolas, and towers, embodied more fully the imposing and ornate Second Empire architecture than any other edifice on the Pacific coast.[15] Baldwin also owned two other California hotels, the Tallac at Lake Tahoe and the Oakwood at Arcadia.

Another popular San Francisco hotel was the long, low

Cliff House, perched on rocks overlooking the Pacific. Opened in 1858 by Samuel Brannan, a wealthy Mormon, it became popular for the view of sea lions romping on the misnamed Seal Rocks. The hotel was the "one special pet dissipation of San Francisco, the very trump card in its hospitality." To drive there through Golden Gate Park with its weekend band concerts and lush gardens was a long-remembered experience. Amused visitors watched the playful sea lions through telescopes and field glasses provided by the house. Described as "uncouth, repulsive amphibia," many of the animals were named for noted Americans—"Ben Butler," "Charles Sumner," and "General Grant," the first because he was such a great beast and the last because he was quiet and slept a great deal.[16] A second Cliff House was built in 1864 after the first burned down, and four years later Rosé Celeste walked a tightrope from its balcony to the Seal Rocks and back, receiving world-wide acclaim. Later purchased by tunnel builder Adolph Sutro, this tourist attraction burned down on Christmas Day, 1894, but was rebuilt again in 1896.

Although San Francisco enjoyed finer hotels than any other Western city, it was not the only town that spent large sums on these establishments. With the Pike's Peak gold rush, the lively town of Denver sprang up a few miles east of the Rocky Mountains, and became a supply center for the miners. The first hotel was the one-story El Dorado, opened in 1859. Another, owned by former mountain man Richens L. "Uncle Dick" Wootton, failed because neither Wootton nor his manager seemed to realize that only paying guests had a right to eat.[17]

The Denver House, another early hotel, was described in 1859 by the irrepressible editor of the New York *Tribune,* Horace Greeley, as "the Astor House of the gold region." This sixty- by thirty-foot house of log walls and dirt floors had windows and roof made of cotton sheeting. In the six apartments there were tin basins which the roomers filled from water barrels placed in the halls; the used water was poured on the earthen floor. At this combination gambling hall-hotel, the irritable Greeley reported that "every guest is allowed as good a bed as his blankets will make." On the third night of his stay, Greeley became angered by the noise of drinking, gambling miners in the front of the house; hauling himself out of bed he limped into the bar and told the boys that he had recently been injured in a stage accident and that their clamor made it impossible for him to sleep. The audience being made to order, Greeley then delivered a lecture adjuring them to abandon their immoral ways and become industrious and worthwhile citizens. He spoke for almost an hour; and his sermon was met with respect from the attentive miners. His first objective was won, for during the remainder of his stay there was no gambling, and the bar was closed every night at eleven.[18]

Criticism did not end with the editor's departure, however. In 1863 a British travel writer found Denver's Tremont House, with Tucker's Celebrated Spring Mattresses on all beds, run on the most democratic principles—the sole qualification for admittance was "being Caucasian." And the bar of the Planter's House reminded a wealthy Londoner, Charles W. Dilke, of a "cockroach corral."[19]

Although at first Denver may have had "the most abominable hotels a person ever put his feet into," later the city could boast of its houses. By 1865 there were twenty-five hotels in Denver. A favorite of foreigners was the City House on Blake Street. There Charles Gleichmann, erstwhile chef to the King of Denmark, was employed. Other good Denver hotels were the 225-room St. James, the 150-room American, and "Delmonico's of the West"—Charpiot's Hotel and Restaurant. But Denver needed more than these for in a three-month period in 1879, 39,000 visitors registered at Denver hotels.

As the number of travelers increased, the need for a family hotel appeared. The problem was quickly solved when a British investment company representative in Denver proposed to his company the idea of building one. The firm agreed and in London in February, 1879, the Denver Mansion Company was incorporated. A Chicago architect planned the hotel to resemble Windsor Castle and the Windsor Hotel of Montreal. Many of the workers on the hotel had to be hired in Chicago as the people of Denver were too busy with other activities. The five-floor, 300-room Windsor, which cost $350,000 to build, was ready June 23, 1880, and proudly displayed Haviland china, furniture from Tobey and W. W. Strong, Reed and Barton silverware, Brussels carpets, three elevators, sixty bathtubs, gas lighting, steam heat, and two artesian wells. Victorian elegance often was measured by the height of ceilings, and the Windsor's were nineteen feet high on the ground floor and eleven and a half on the fifth floor. For fire safety "mercurial alarms" had been set in the ceiling of each room and, if the temperature got above 120°, the desk was notified. In such emergencies there was fire equipment on each floor and water stored on the roof.

The English hotel company turned over the management to the Colorado firm of Bush, Tabor, and Hall, which furnished it for $200,000. (The Bush in this trio was the same William Bush who had run the Teller and Clarendon hotels. Some years later he opened the Brown Palace in Denver.) Across an alley from the hotel and connected by a tunnel was the "Little Windsor," a three-story, fifty-room edifice for the staff, which numbered 154 employees, one of whom was head bartender Harry H. Tammen, who later owned the Denver *Post* and the Sells-Floto Circus.[20]

Even as late as 1885, however, an English guest wrote of primitive conditions in a Denver hotel. "The creatures that attacked us were not fleas, something worse. . . . They were in dozens on the whitewashed walls, and running all over the beds." He was forced to spend the night on a table in the bar, and the next morning complained to the landlord about the bugs. The publican indignantly retorted that, while some of the insects perhaps came with the place, the guest probably brought most of them.[21]

Cheyenne was typical of early Western hotel development. When the town was founded in 1867, Foster Zincke took a room there, but the din of gamblers in the adjoining chamber was so loud that he stopped up a hole in the wall with a Chicago newspaper. Although his window could be opened easily from the outside, he felt safe since the town's vigilantes had hanged two lawbreakers a few nights earlier. Nevertheless, the overly cautious landlord sent an employee to his room the next morning to make sure that none of the blankets had been stolen.

A year later, Loreta Janeta Velazquez stopped at the Cheyenne House. This unusual woman, who had participated in the Civil War by dressing as a man, using the name Harry T. Buford, and wearing the Union Blue, called the Cheyenne House "the worst apology for a hotel" she had ever seen in her travels. The small bedrooms were separated by canvas partitions. Beds were for two; mattresses and pillows were made of flour bags stuffed with straw; blankets were gray, with "U. S. A." plainly marked on them. The floor was made of rough pine boards and, worst of all, she was forced to share a bed with a drunken woman.[22]

The Salt Lake House was the first hotel in prosperous and placid Salt Lake City. In the late summer of 1860 Richard Burton described it simply as a two-story wooden building opposite the post office, with a corral in the backyard. Burton, looking for the bar, passed some rough-looking men in the doorway, but proceeded upstairs, where he espied a ballroom, a well-furnished parlor, and partitioned bedrooms.[23] Burton considered landlord James E. Townsend, a Mormon from Maine, to be in the "highest degree civil and obliging," for he was often able to arrange interviews with Brigham Young for his guests. Townsend and his English-born second wife made Burton's three-week stay a pleasant and illuminating one. Discussing with him the history of the Mormons, Burton learned of their trials after being expelled from Nauvoo, Illinois, in 1846. Nevertheless, Burton objected to certain unsanitary aspects of the house such as the "emigration flies" which appeared in September with the emigrants, lived for a month, and died with the first snow.[24]

In 1865 Townsend sold the hotel to Brigham Young for

$25,000 and moved to England for three years to gather Mormon converts. The humorist Artemus Ward joked that he didn't know how effective Townsend was as an exponent of Mormonism, but his beefsteaks and chicken pies were delicious. The monetary-minded Young placed one of his many relatives, Feramorz Little, as host and, to obtain more money from the gentiles or non-Mormons, opened a bar in the house where "valley tan," the Mormon distilled whiskey, was dispensed with alacrity to thirsty travelers.

After proselytizing in England, Townsend returned to Salt Lake City and opened another hotel, the Townsend House. Here, however, he seemed to have lost the cordiality which Burton had noted. In this "abominable" place, an Austrian diplomat observed that non-Mormons were looked upon with unfriendly eyes by Townsend, who paid little attention to his house and less to his roomers, leaving the work to his three wives. For hours he would spend his time in "sublime contemplation," lying back in a chair on the veranda, regarding his feet. William F. Rae, a correspondent for the London *Daily News,* stopping there in 1869, concluded that if one had an enemy he would like to torture, he should send him to the Townsend in the fall, where the flies would worry him to death.[25]

By the late 1870's, Salt Lake had four adequate hotels: the Townsend, the Salt Lake, the Revere, and the Walker; the first two were run by Mormons, while the latter two were managed by gentiles. The Walker, owned by an ex-Mormon, provided bathtubs, Hess electric bells to call the desk, gas heat, and other modern conveniences. Among the special services the Walker offered its guests was "a competent guide

free of charge, to conduct them to all places of interests in
the city, introduce them to prominent personages when required, and give all needed information."[26]

Omaha, following the Western pattern in building too
many hotels, wanted "to run before she could walk." The
St. Nicholas was the community's first hotel in 1854. A year
later, the two-story Douglas House opened; George A. Sala,
a journalist for the London *Daily Telegraph*, reported that
it was such a "high-toned" place that it would have been
considered a decided breach of etiquette to shoot the bartender for refusing credit.[27] Another early hotel was the
four-story, brick Herndon, built in 1857 and named after the
Amazon explorer William L. Herndon. The Herndon was
too large for the town and in 1870 was occupied by the
offices of the Union Pacific Railroad. Five years later, the
house was purchased by the railroad for $42,000.

The voluble George Francis Train, promoter extraordi-
nary, roomed at the Herndon and one day in May, 1867, gave
a breakfast in the dining room for some prominent friends.
During the Western meal of Nebraska trout and prairie
chicken, a cyclonic storm shook the hotel and broke a window
near their table. Train paid a Negro waiter ten cents a
minute to stand with his back to the window. The manager
angered Train by requesting the waiter to go back to work.
When the atmospheric storm passed, the incensed Train left
the hotel and purchased a vacant lot across the street for
$5,000. He hired a builder at $1,000 a day and drew on the
back of an envelope a rough design of his proposed three-
story hotel. Train told the builder he was leaving town but

that a 120-room hotel should be finished when he returned in sixty days. It was, and he leased it to a Mr. Cozzens of West Point, New York, for $10,500 a year.[28]

In 1870 an English major arrived in Omaha and went to the Cozzens', which was the best hotel in town at that time. "The best" left much to be desired as the Britisher soon learned when he asked an attendant if he could take a bath and he was told that the hotel had no tubs. Fortunately, in anticipation of such an emergency, the major had brought along his India-rubber tub. The Englishman discovered that at the Cozzens' if one stayed in the "ruck of feeding times, and don't want to splash" he would get along fine; but an unhappy visit would follow if one asked for too much and got out of the "course of events."[29] In 1871 the Cozzens' closed for a time and another hotel was started by a citizens' stock company. Costing over $300,000, the Grand Central was opened in September, 1873. George Thrall was the first manager and lessee. Born in Rutland, Vermont, in 1836, he had worked as clerk in New Orleans and St. Louis hostelries, but even with this background, Thrall could not keep the five-story house from running in the red. In 1878 fire solved the hotel's economic problems.

These early hotels were typical of Western boisterousness, optimism, and hopefulness. As more and more Easterners and Europeans came and criticized their caravansaries, Western hotelmen decided that their houses could achieve respectability and success by copying the established Eastern hotels. When they reached that goal, however, and emulated the sophistication of the East, the houses had lost most of their early captivating charm.

71

[5]

Resort Hotels

REFINEMENTS IN TRAIN ACCOMMODATIONS AND THE appearance of conducted tours brought tourists west. With their coming, resort hotels appeared in California in the late 1870's and 1880's on the sandy slopes of the Pacific. They resembled such elegant Eastern resorts as the 2,000-bed Grand Union at Saratoga Springs and the Grand Central at White Sulphur Springs. Well-to-do Easterners were becoming jaded by Atlantic coast hotels, which, moreover, were being invaded by the general populace. The new Western hotels, because they were distant and dear, kept the masses out. Enormous and expensive, they catered to those pleasure-seekers who traveled thousands of miles westward to enjoy sunshine and relaxation, and gave to areas lingering in a rural lethargy "a curious urban overtone of sophistication." Lectures on Shakespeare, butterflies, geology, archaeology, and biology were popular with culture-conscious guests.

While much of the West was still endangered by Indians

and outlaws, tourist hotels offered to their guests comforts and sights found nowhere else in the United States. So the tourists paid their money, proceeded on a week's train ride in a plush car, spied a few gaunt Indians and herds of indifferent cattle from a respectable distance, and lodged at these ornate hostelries.

With the opening on February 27, 1876, of the ninety-room Arlington in languorous Santa Barbara, the California tourist-hotel era began. This $170,000 three-story house was erected by a company headed by Ohio-born sheep rancher, Colonel William W. Hollister. Every room was appointed with running water, gaslights, marble-mantled fireplaces, and annunciators (a mechanical device invented by Seth Fuller to signal the desk for service). The furnishings cost $30,000 and were purchased by Mrs. Hollister in San Francisco. In order to stimulate business Hollister hired Dixie W. Thompson as manager. The new host's popularity was exceeded only by his ability to plan lavish entertainment for his guests —picnics on the yellow beach at Castle Rock, horseback rides along shaded paths, flora and fauna expeditions, visits to the friendly padres at Santa Barbara Mission, and tallyho rides over San Marcos Pass for a view of the softly blue Santa Barbara Valley. Thompson urged his invalid guests to swim in the Pacific with his query, "Did you ever see a sailor with a cold?" As Hollister began to reap a harvest from this cash crop of tourists, others were entering the tourist-hotel business.

With empty Southern Pacific Railroad coaches running south of San Jose, one of the road's owners, rotund Charles Crocker, decided that the best way to attract visitors to that area, and make a sound financial investment as well, was to construct on Monterey Bay a luxurious year-round resort hotel. The Pacific Improvement Company, the railroad's construction subsidiary, raised the three-story Del Monte, which in June, 1880, was opened with all the pomp indispensable for such an occasion. This $250,000 achievement, with an all-white interior and vestiges of Saratoga and Hampton Court, was reckoned by some to be "Crocker's Folly." A Boston suffragette fancied the building was so large (it could accommodate 400 guests) that it would be fifty years before the needs of the region would equal the capacity of the Del Monte.[1] She was proven wrong as newer, swifter trains such as the "Del Monte Limited" brought Monterey within three and one-half hours of San Francisco. The hotel's success was further assured when high society decreed that residing at the Del Monte was only for the socially prominent.

Not all were pleased by the changes the hotel made in the community, for Robert Louis Stevenson wrote:[2]

> Alas for the little town! it is not strong enough to resist the influence of the flaunting caravanserai, and the poor, quaint, penniless native gentlemen of Monterey must perish, like a lower race, before the millionaire vulgarians of the Big Bonanza.

The Southern Pacific spared neither effort nor words to bring the traveling public to the Del Monte. According to a prospectus put out some years after the hotel opened, its purpose was "to provide the best means of deriving the highest benefits from the natural charms of California." The pamphlet offered guests "a new and strange world, which sets aside

74

familiar experiences and invites to a study of life from a novel point of view."[3]

In the latter part of the nineteenth century, it was common to read in hotel prospectuses laudatory comments by distinguished people from many walks of life. Chicago businessman Andrew McNally of Rand McNally considered the Del Monte the *"ne plus ultra"*; Joseph Pulitzer reported it was not to be equaled; and a doctor, C. B. Currier, declared that, for a winter resort, it was "incomparable."

If guests sought activity, the Del Monte had much to offer them. For three dollars a day or $17.50 a week vacationers could indulge in such sports as tennis, shuffleboard on the veranda, bowling at five cents a game and, for the more adventurous, a race track and polo grounds. Giddy guests splashed in the Pacific and bloomer-clad women frolicked on the white sand beaches, where a more daring bather might wear her new Paris creation—a "cross between Mme. Dockrill's circus habiliments and Aphrodite's"—or rent one for twenty-five cents. If the weather was intemperate, there were four large indoor swimming pools filled daily with ocean water, each heated at a different temperature. Those who did not care to swim could walk about the magnificent grounds or stroll across the lobby, which was much like that of the Grand Union at Saratoga Springs. Others sat "indolently in the easiest of lolling and lazy" chairs on the shaded veranda and eyed newcomers with an air of superior wisdom, if only because they had arrived earlier. When Ballenberg's band played for summer dances, the latest creations of New York and Paris *couturières* were on display.[4]

At the Del Monte women were given more freedom of

above, HOTEL DEL
MONTE, MONTEREY,
CALIFORNIA; *left,*
BALDWIN HOTEL, SAN
FRANCISCO, CALIFOR-
NIA, 1890'S

(Bancroft Library, University of California)

movement than was usually found in Victorian hotels, where separate entrances and special dining rooms were some of the devices used to separate the sexes. With access to all public rooms, the women also had a billiard room for their own use. Susie C. Clark, a traveler from Boston, remarked that in comparison with the Del Monte, everything else was unimportant. Recognizing the inadequacy of her vocabulary to depict its beauty, she rhapsodized: "The nights are a blank, a refreshing plunge in Lethean oblivion until the birds with enticing call lure us to an early walk beneath the umbrageous shades which they have chosen to inhabit." If Paradise were fairer, she hoped Death would not delay too long.[5]

To achieve its splendor and elegance, forty gardeners took immaculate care of the 126 acres of Monterey pine, live oak, walnut, spruce, cypress, and exotic flowers. This floral labyrinth, modeled on England's Hampton Court, was surrounded by ten-foot-high hedgerows. One section of the garden, which contained only cacti, was named "Arizona." The garden's twisted somber cypresses gave the place a foreign air. European influence was further felt when those who could not find rooms in the main building, whose architectural style was labeled Swiss Gothic, were lodged at one of the small wooden Swiss cottages.

The hotel overlooked 7,000 acres of land; and a guest could cycle, enjoy a boat cruise on Laguna del Rey, take a carriage trip to Cypress Point, Carmel Mission, and Point Lobos, or be driven along the beach on the macadamized Seventeen-Mile Drive, where squirrels, pheasants, and deer might be seen scampering in the distance.

On April 1, 1887, the hotel was gutted by fire. William

Randolph Hearst, new owner of the San Francisco *Examiner*, was not to be outdone by the other San Francisco papers in the coverage of this calamity. Impatient to make his journalistic mark, Hearst chartered a Southern Pacific train and, with a full entourage of writers and artists, sped down to Monterey. Out of this effort came a fourteen-page special fire edition on April 3, which read like a detective story and circus spectacle rolled into one.[6] This was the first in a long line of Hearstian newspaper extravaganzas.

Railroads were often helpful to the hotel industry. Pasadena became a booming town in 1885 with the coming of the San Gabriel Valley Railroad. Three years earlier, thirty-year-old Walter Raymond visited Pasadena as a guide for a tourist party. Unable to find suitable accommodations and recognizing the town's future importance, Raymond decided to build a tourist hotel. He was the son of Emmons Raymond, senior partner of the Boston-based Raymond and Whitcomb Travel Agency. This recently formed company reportedly gave to the excursionist "a mind absolutely free from care about your destination or your belongings." Using snob appeal, the company advertised the opportunity for its patrons to mingle with others of the "refined and cultured" class. They stayed in the best hotels, ate at the better restaurants, and knew from the start the exact expense; Mary E. Blake, a Boston mother of eleven children, wrote that there was no better way by which one could take such a trip so pleasantly.[7] Besides taking the hurry and worry out of travel, one of the main reasons for the popularity of these tours was the fact that they gave the vacationer a feeling of security and isola-

tion from the rest of the world. Organized tours were no help
to the independent traveler, however. He arrived at his hotel
only to find the rooms already occupied by members of a
tour and the tourists themselves noisily relaxing in the lobby
and dining rooms.

Hotel coupons were sold to excursionists who planned to
stay longer than the regular tour, the advantage being that it
was a less expensive way to room and usually gave the holder
better treatment and accommodations. Coupons not used could
be redeemed at full value. Two forms were sold—A and B;
the former was more expensive and was good for rooms on
the higher-priced lower floors. With the appearance of elevators such price distinctions ceased.[8]

In November, 1883, Walter Raymond began construction
of his hotel on Bacon's Hill in East Pasadena, but financial
difficulties halted the building. His father, aware of the approaching railroad, came to his aid with more capital, and
the $400,000 Raymond opened brilliantly on November 17,
1886, with 35,000 guests the first year. The 200-room hotel
was open from autumn to spring and the Raymond and Whitcomb tours were an ever-present feature. The Raymond was
operated in conjunction with the Crawford House in New
Hampshire's White Mountains, and several hundred employees from the Crawford were moved to the Raymond in
the fall. It was advertised that one could leave a snowstorm
in Boston and, in a few days, find oneself in a "Boston hotel
in Paradise." On Sunday mornings church buses arrived at
the hotel, and the doorman directed traffic, yelling, "Presby-
terians this way; Episcopalians here; Methodists in the blue
bus; Unitarians along here; Congregationalists this way."[9]

A Raymond prospectus reported that each "improvement that modern hotel science could suggest, or money supply, has been introduced, and the result has been such as to meet every possible requirement." As another attraction for the hotel the management hired the well-known naturalist and sportsman, Charles Frederick Holder, as author-in-residence to write books, articles, pamphlets, and to give lectures on the wonders of Pasadena and the glories of the Raymond. In pursuing his publicity campaign to attract tourists, Holder founded the New Year's Day Tournament of Roses Parade in 1890. With playgrounds, tennis courts, coach rides, and bridle paths, the house provided for its guests a variety of outdoor recreations over its fifty-five acres. And from the veranda guests could gaze at the lovely San.Gabriel Valley and the hotel gardens, where "Brilliancy, color and fragrance are everywhere at high tide."[10] The hotel maintained this magnificence until April, 1895, when the Raymond burned to the ground.

Southern California was, in part, an illusion created by long-winded, prevaricating publicists, but it was profitable from a businessman's point of view. Nothing, however, gave witness to the stability and future prosperity of the region more than its huge, new hotels. Most of these were exclusive and followed the Eastern pattern of refined living with wide balconies, long porches, ornate furniture, numerous employees, and magnificent views of the ocean and mountains. Thanks to an abundance of letters, books, and newspaper accounts, by the 1880's many Americans supposed that southern California's climate could cure most ills. Among those caught up in this "health rush" was Elisha S. Babcock, Jr., of Evansville, Indiana, who in 1884 came for a health-seeking vacation to San Diego, where there were already a number of hotels. San Diego's consummate town promoter, Alonzo E. Horton, owned the 100-room, brick Horton House, which had opened in 1870 at a cost of $150,000. The city also boasted another hotel, the Florence, whose manager's smile was considered "appetizing, and his table is a feast."[11]

With a Chicago friend, Babcock took a boat ride over to the rabbit-infested peninsula later named Coronado. While strolling on the beach, he conceived the idea of building a damn-the-cost, splendid resort hotel which would attract tourists from all over the world. The Coronado Beach Company was formed to purchase and develop the peninsula and build the hotel. A successful grocer and hardware merchant, Babcock knew the value of advertising and spent thousands of dollars throughout the country on a publicity campaign.

The Del Coronado was constructed by two Evansville architects, James W. and Merritt J. Reid, using unskilled Chinese labor and lumber from San Francisco, in the common Queen Anne or Elizabethan Cottage style. Perched roofs, long porches, and towers made it especially suitable as a resort hotel, as did its alfresco sleeping areas, galleries, and glass-enclosed verandas.

Opened on February 14, 1888, as a year-round resort it was an instant success; one Englishwoman, Mrs. Edward H. Carbutt, on a trip to the United States in 1888, even suspected that it was to be used as a lure to attract settlers and speculators. Praising this 750-room hotel, which provided wall safes and fireplaces in every suite and seventeen and a half acres of carpet, a pamphlet puffed it as a grand edifice of Oriental brilliance. It was built around an inner court where the sun "has full play on the tender leaves of the rare exotics, on the chaste statuary." There were thirty billiard tables (four for ladies), four eighty-five-foot bowling alleys, a dark room for camera buffs, and a De Coppet absorption machine which made ice in fifteen hours for those who cared to wait.[12]

The famous actress, Lily Langtry, declared that the hotel's "immensity astonishes me, and its perfect beauty delights me." Moreover, it gave her an impression of "pleasing repose and altogether it has a delightful influence on me." A health-seeking physician remarked that cholera infantum and other childhood diseases were not present there.[13]

At that time, the Del Coronado had the largest incandescent lighting plant in the West with 2,500 lights; Thomas Alva Edison came to the hotel to oversee its installation. Most of the 300 employees came by rail from the East. The wood-paneled, 1,000-seat dining room had a floor space of 10,000 feet without pillar or post and a thirty-three-foot high ceiling. The American merchant and editor, Charles Dudley Warner, affirmed that the hotel was an "airy and pictuesque and half-bizarre wooden creation." To Susie Clark it appeared to be the palace of Aladdin.[14] To many it was a dream come true. Fleeing from the hardness and corruption of a plutocratic age, tourists were ferried over from San Diego to play at this cloudland caravansary where thoughts of their uncertain to-morrows were displaced by scenic vistas, comforts, and repose.

While the Southwest did not have as many resort hotels as California, one that stood out was the Montezuma Hot

Springs Hotel, six miles north of Las Vegas, New Mexico. A pioneer in the tourist industry in that territory, it was built and run by the Las Vegas Hot Springs Company, a subsidiary of the Atchison, Topeka and Santa Fe Railroad. Opening on April 7, 1882, the house held the customary banquet and dance, with music provided by Professor Helm's Fourth Cavalry Orchestra. Four days before the gala, Clark D. Frost, former manager of the Lindell in St. Louis, arrived with fifty-four employees.[15] Thus the house had a well-trained staff when it opened. Raiding superior hotels in Chicago, St. Louis, New York, and other large cities for managers and staffs was a fairly common procedure to enable a new house to start with experienced employees.

The building of 300 rooms displayed Axminster rugs, marble fireplaces, oak paneling, an aviary, a menagerie, a casino seating 1,000, and a well-stocked wine cellar. Although the prospectus proudly boasted that because of the number of fire hoses and pipes it was practically inconceivable for a fire to cause serious damage or to get beyond the room in which it started, on January 8, 1884, a fire broke out and the hotel was destroyed.[16] When not fighting the blaze, firemen crowded into the cellar to swill wine.

When the second Montezuma, or Phoenix Hotel, opened a year later, a guest could feast on savory dishes prepared under the supervision of that Lucullus of the West, Fred Harvey, who kept several refrigerator cars busy hauling in fresh food; Harvey was supplied every week by Yaqui Indians with four live green turtles, twenty pounds of celery, and sea bass. The bathhouses could accommodate 1,000 bathers daily, and offered a choice of douche, electric, medicated, vapor, shampoo, tub, spray, shower, or ring bath. Again, however, fire struck, and the Phoenix was destroyed. Another hotel was built in 1886; its opening was attended by the aged frontiersman, Alexander W. Doniphan, who wrote his daughter that the new house was beautiful "in all its design and furnish."[17]

A more successful resort area was Colorado Springs, Colorado. Before the tourists and health seekers came, a middle-aged British financial writer, James Burnley, stayed at one of the town's hotels, where he heard men talking of lawlessness. He tried to explain to the attendant, who was "deaf as a door-nail," what type of room he wanted; but the best he could get was a small room, where he spent a sleepless night. As more people stopped off at Colorado Springs to partake of the dry climate and scenic beauties, the townspeople decided to build a first-class hotel. Early in 1881 railroad builder General William Jackson Palmer promised to put up $25,000 if the townspeople added an equal amount. The terms were met and first mortgage bonds totaling $50,000 were issued. A hotel company was organized with capital of $100,000 "to erect, construct [of lava stone], equip, furnish, maintain, and operate a first class hotel." The opening of the $125,000 Antlers in June, 1883, was an occasion for a grand celebration; dignitaries attended from New York, Boston, and London.[18]

Hotels of the resort-recreation type were established in the parks of the West. In 1872, when the area was made a national park, Yellowstone hotels were put under the control of the Secretary of the Interior. Until 1890, when it, too, became a national park, the hostels in Yosemite were run by the state of California. By 1890 at Yellowstone there were seven hotels; the largest and best-known was that "huge yel-

HOTEL DEL CORONADO, CORONADO, CALIFORNIA

(Bancroft Library, University of California)

MONTEZUMA HOT SPRINGS HOTEL, NEAR LAS VEGAS, NEW MEXICO

(Santa Fe Railway)

low barn," the Mammoth Hot Springs. Built in 1884 and furnished for $60,000, this comfortable four-story house had accommodations for over 500 guests. Other park hotels were the Norris Geyser, Lower Geyser, Upper Geyser, and Shoshone Lake. Because all the hostels were under the same management, a visitor was given a letter of credit upon entering the park and did not pay any bills until he or she left. An English woman, Emily C. Bates, who traveled in the West in 1886, noted that the only drawbacks in Yellowstone houses were the terrible food and the maddening perseverance of enormous mosquitoes.[19]

Yosemite's first hotel, the Lower House, opened in 1857; two years later the Upper House was ready for business. By the end of the 1860's the hotels in the then state park were important to California's economy. In 1864, author-publisher James M. Hutchings, who was in the first tourist party to Yosemite in 1855, purchased the Upper House. Hutchings had had the house for ten years when he sold it to the state of California for $24,000.[20]

This two-story frame building with a "soft finish" of white muslin and cotton cloth had doors made of slats. A British author of numerous travel books believed that a strong wind would blow it down. Because the walls were cloth, guests were forced to extinguish their candles before disrobing, unless they wished to give undressing displays. Hutchings was an absent-minded hotelkeeper, for one guest mentioned the time that he forgot the knives and forks, and gave sugar to guests who requested salt. Even the kindly Sara Jane Lippincott, a New York writer, maintained that he was not "high-toned on grub," and believed there were better things for him to do. Ralph Waldo Emerson, visiting the West in the spring of 1871, stopped in Yosemite and was entertained by Hutchings with California wines and stories of the Digger Indians.[21]

Another house, opened in 1857, was run by Galen Clark; when Clark sold a half interest to Edwin Moore in 1870, it was known as Clark and Moore's. That long, log house, like other park hotels, opened in May and closed the first of November. One guest held that Clark was a "modern anchorite —a hater of civilization and a lover of the forest—handsome, thoughtful, interesting, and slovenly." Somewhat like Louis Dupuy, Clark was philosopher, scholar, geologist, landlord, and chef. Another visitor concluded that, while Clark's was located in a picturesque spot, it was poorly managed, too expensive ($4.50 a day), and served inferior victuals.[22] A Yosemite house, also scenically situated, was Macaulay's on Glacier Point. To get into the bedrooms it was necessary to climb a ladder; if a guest misstepped, it was a 3,000-foot drop to the valley below.

The cost of a room at Yosemite hotels in the early 1870's was $3.50 a day and, since the nearest town was forty miles away, such charges were reasonable. The rooms were usually clean, the food passable and, if there were no bathtubs, the same could be said for many city hotels. These houses were built not to live in but to sleep in, for it was felt that the guest would be roaming through the park most of the day and would reappear only to eat and sleep. For such arrangements, these park hotels were suitable, even if the landlords were inept and, on occasion, dangerous. At Leidig's, Arthur Vivian remarked, the host, George F. Leidig, was so happy to see his customer that he decided to explode a dynamite cartridge. Vivian became frightened when the landlord began to thaw out a frozen cartridge under the stove. The Britisher pointed out that everyone might be blown up. But when the charge was ready the proprietor hastily withdrew, and a few minutes later Vivian, with great relief, heard the explosion; the danger was over.[23]

[6]

Hotelmen and Employees

THE INFLUENCE OF WESTERN HOTEL PROPRIETORS WAS
considerable, for the success or failure of many new towns
depended upon their hotels. Townspeople knew that most
prosperous communities had good to excellent hotels; to the
Westerner an able hotelman meant a well-run hotel, which,
in turn, meant a thriving town. If a community had a successful hotel, the future would take care of itself; and, if it had
more than one important house, there was bound to be a
wonderful boom.

Providing the necessities of life to hungry, thirsty, and
tired cowboys, miners, and travelers, the innovating proprietor also brought what few comforts there were to the bleak
wasteland. In that simple age and distant area, anyone who
was able to manage a multifaceted institution and furnish
it with crystal chandeliers, mahogany bars, and plush carpets
was judged a success. Thus the confident hotel proprietor represented excellent administrative ability. "You're a pretty

good fellow but you can't keep a hotel" meant that, even though a man might have business acumen, he didn't necessarily have that special and rare talent possessed by successful hotelkeepers. Because of the complexity of a hotel operation, it was often remarked that only "born fools and educated idiots" chose the career.

Hotelmen were an aggregate of all types—former fur trappers, stage drivers, cowmen, miners, and ministers. Some, unused to their new importance, became impressed with themselves, demanding from their employees and preferring from their customers the appellations of "colonel" and "major," while a guest was often addressed by landlords as "man," and "fellow." The constantly complaining Mrs. Edward Carbutt reported that she had met several owners who were happy to discuss the weather and politics, but who considered such matters as carriage prices or business beneath their dignity. Typical of a self-satisfied landlord was the one Edmond Mandat-Grancey came upon in a Dakota hotel. Propped up behind his desk, fatigued from the day's labors, the "kind of colossus embellished with formidable moustaches" pushed the register toward his guest without disturbing his sublime repose. It was all he could do to summon a porter to show the Frenchman his quarters.[1]

On the other hand, many owners showed concern and friendliness toward their guests and attempted to do all that was possible to make their stay comfortable. At the better hotels the art of hospitality was assiduously practiced. The courteous, personal service in such cities as San Francisco, St. Louis, and Denver was as fine as anything offered in the East.

But the extremes of hotelmanship in the West were astonishing.

In the smaller Western hotels the landlord and his family divided the work. The wife cooked and made the beds; the husband was clerk and bartender; and the children cleaned the house, took care of guests' horses, cleaned the stable, and learned the business. In the larger hotels the proprietor hired employees with specialized skills who were often undependable and extremely independent, and some said that staffs became more haughty and rude as one went westward.

If travelers stayed at enough Western hotels, they encountered the entire range of landlords. The well-traveled Presbyterian parson, John Brown, who spent twenty-five years in the West, observed that Texas hotelkeepers feared neither God nor man. During many a long restless night Brown wished that he was on the highest peak of the Rocky Mountains, instead of in a Texas hotel. One of those nights, in a Texas backwash, the parson stopped at a hotel kept by an odd, elderly couple, one puffing a corncob pipe, the other dipping snuff. Perhaps wondering why any honest person would be in such a remote region, the old hag inquired if he had committed a crime. Parson Brown indignantly responded that he was a man of the cloth, at which the harridan screeched, "Then pay your bill and go up-sta'rs."[2]

An unusual landlord named Peers ran a hotel in Fort Worth. This dignified gentleman, a young guest reported, had an imagination which, like Texas, was "vast, if not limitless." Peers asserted that in addition to owning the hotel, he was America's greatest Greek scholar. Furthermore, he had

91

financed the Mexican War, had been the chief Confederate spy, and had saved General Robert E. Lee from a rout at Gettysburg by serving a watermelon to General Winfield S. Hancock, who consequently became too stuffed to attack, letting Lee slip away.[3]

The practices of some hotelmen made their guests uncomfortable and unhappy. A landlord in Leadville, without enough blankets to go around, contrived a money-saving scheme: if a guest complained about the lack of blankets in his room, the apologetic host explained there had been so much thievery lately that he was afraid to leave bedding in the rooms, but would get a blanket from the storeroom. Instead, he gently removed one from an occupied bed and gave it to the complaining guest. Unfortunately for him, his shivering roomers caught on and tied the blankets to the bedposts, eventually forcing this penurious proprietor out of business.[4]

In that predetergent age, dirt was a problem in Western hotels. If a guest grumbled about the filth, a landlord could do one of three things—remove it, ignore it, or make a joke of it. After entering his room in a Washington Territory hotel, a boarder came quickly back to the office hollering that the pillowcase and sheets were filthy. The amazed landlord exclaimed to this roomer that a hundred men had slept in that bed and he was the first to complain.[5]

The revolver played a prominent role in the West, and it was not healthy for a landlord to be curt with a guest. A German hotelkeeper in the Northwest was shot and killed while trying to stop a drunken brawl. In Albuquerque, New Mexico, the Exchange Hotel was run by an obnoxious fellow,

Tom Post. When a guest found fault with the soiled linen, Post nonchalantly retorted that it was changed regularly once a year, whereupon the traveler muttered that an Indian tepee would have been more pleasant. As agent for a stage company, Post was in a position to make it bothersome to those staying at rival houses by refusing them a seat on the stage. Told this once too often, a salesman warned Post that, if he did not find him a seat, the stage company would be minus an agent. The quick-tempered drummer was soon on his way.[6]

Conversely, it could be equally hazardous to antagonize a Western landlord, for a German tavernkeeper in Missouri shot a drunken Frenchman who had annoyed him. Another incident involving an armed landlord occurred when a guest, in order to catch an early morning train, left a 2:00 A.M. call with the owner, whereupon the obliging fellow stayed up all night to wake his boarder. When called, however, the man mumbled sleepily that he had changed his mind and decided to stay. The angered proprietor ordered him to get on the train or he would shoot off his head.[7] The guest caught the train. On another occasion, after a few murders had been committed in northern California, hotelmen formed a vigilante committee and marched all suspicious characters out of the neighborhood at gunpoint, warning them that they would be hanged if they returned.

Bills were often the cause of disputes. A tenderfoot at a Deadwood hotel told the landlord that $4.50 for dinner was too high. Fingering the handle of his gun, the host replied that it might be, but he needed the money. He got it. Two more incidents of acutely enraged landlords took place in a

"A HOME FOR THE BOYS"

(from Browne, *Adventures in the Apache Country*, Lilly Library)

Texas hotel and at a Missouri tavern. When a guest refused to pay his bill in the former, the owner beat him over the head with a cane; in the latter, when a commercial traveler complained about the food, the owner called him a "blamed skunk" and kicked him out of the house.[8]

The Western hotel was one of the few businesses that employed Negroes. And there were a few Negro landlords in the West who ran good houses. B. L. Ford of Cheyenne, Wyoming, was a well-known Negro hotelkeeper who owned two of that town's finest hotels, the Ford House and the three-story Inter-Ocean. Samuel Bowles, an influential Massachusetts newspaper editor, met a Negro who owned a comfortable hotel in Olympia, Washington. Fifty years old and weighing 300 pounds, that boniface served the distinguished editor excellent meals with refinement and dignity.[9]

There were a number of women hotelkeepers in the West, usually widows, who sometimes ran cleaner and more comfortable, if smaller, hotels than their male counterparts. Not all services performed by these women were limited to their notices, however. An Irish landlady who managed the Apache Hotel in Holbrook, Arizona, one night found that a guest from Texas had been shot in the foot by a Mexican and needed a doctor. With pot-valiant Mexicans outside thirsting for more blood, she bravely made her way to the doctor's office, woke him, and brought him back to her hotel. Fully aware of imminent danger, she had cautiously placed a Colt revolver under her apron. In a San Angelo, Texas, hotel a rancher who had killed a drunken Negro soldier looked out the window to see Negro soldiers coming for him. The dauntless landlady of the establishment took her shotgun and went out to meet them with the warning "Cut it out. The first one that shoots a hole in my hotel, I'm going to kill him." No shots were fired.[10]

Ireland-born Nellie Cashman operated the Russ House in Tombstone, Arizona, in the early 1880's. Before arriving in Tombstone, "Aunt Nell" had managed boardinghouses and restaurants in mining camps throughout the West and Canada, and was admired and loved for the help she gave anyone in need. One day a drummer loudly complained to this "Angel of Tombstone" about the quality of beans he was served. A miner drew his gun, stalked over to the salesman's table, and ordered, "Stranger . . . eat them beans." Assuming an expression of pure delight, he downed every one.

Not all landladies were held in high esteem. "Mother Damnable" ran Seattle's first hotel, the Falker House, where she kept three mongrels to attack offending roomers and sometimes, with her apron filled with sticks and rocks, pelted and cursed lodgers from the premises. Frontiersman Thomas Henry Tibbles encountered a surly female proprietor at a Caldwell, Kansas, hotel. Sick from bad water, he stopped at her dingy house. After Tibbles was visited by a doctor, she returned and told him he must leave because the doctor said he was going to die and "I ain't got no time ter wait on yer, an' if yer die on me here, yer'll hurt my business fer weeks."[11]

To attract customers, Western hotel owners advertised a good deal. Most handbills and ads were boring and repetitious, but there were exceptions. A Phoenix hotel boasted that it was the "Only House in the City Employing White Labor Throughout," and a few years earlier, another had stated that it was the "Only Hotel in Phoenix." One attracted roomers with "Customers in possession of Bedding will be *Lodged Free of Charge.*"[12] But most houses repeated ad nauseam "rebuilt and refinished," "the largest and best," "cheapest and best," "hotel being entirely new," or "hotel has undergone thorough repairs." One Wyoming landlord humorously specified that, if the location was inconvenient, he would have the hotel moved.

One form of advertising was disappointing to an English tourist who saw the grandeur of Utah's Echo Canyon dimin-

THE
DESERT HOUSE
Green River City, Wyoming Territory.

This hotel has been built and arranged for the special comfort and convenience of summer boarders. On arrival each guest will be asked how he likes the situation; and if he says the hotel ought to have been placed up upon the knoll, or further down toward the village, the location of the house will be immediately changed. Corner front rooms, up only one flight, for every guest.

Baths, gas, ~~~~~~~ hot and cold water, laundry, telegraph, restaurant, fire alarm, bar room, billiard table, daily papers, coupe, sewing machine, grand piano, a clergyman, and all other modern conveniences, in every room. Meals every minute if desired, and, consequently, no second table. English, French and German dictionaries furnished every guest, to make up such a bill-of-fare as he may desire, without regard to the bill-affair afterward at the office. Waiters of any nationality and color desired. Every waiter furnished with a libretto, button-hole bouquet, full-dress suits, ball-tablets, and his hair parted in the middle. Every guest will have the best seat in the dining hall, and the best waiter in the house.

Any guest not getting his breakfast red-hot, or experiencing a delay of sixteen seconds after giving his order for dinner, will please mention the fact at the office, and the cooks and waiters will be blown from the mouth of the cannon in front of the hotel at once. Children will be welcomed with delight, and are requested to bring hoop-sticks and haw-keys to bang the carved rosewood furniture especially provided for that purpose, and peg-tops to spin on the velvet carpets; they will be allowed to bang on the piano at all hours, yell in the halls, slide down the bannisters, fall down stairs, carry away dessert enough for a small family in their pockets at dinner, and make themselves as disagreeable as the fondest mother can desire.

Washing allowed in rooms, and ladies giving an order to "put me on a flat-iron" will be put on one at any hour of the day or night. A discreet waiter, who belongs to the Masons, Odd Fellows, Knights of Pythias, and who was never known to even tell the time of day, has been employed to carry milk punches and hot toddies to ladies' rooms in the evening.

Every lady will be considered the belle of the house, and row-boys will answer the belle promptly. Should any row-boy fail to appear at a guest's door with a pitcher of ice water, more towels, a gin cocktail, and pen, ink and paper, before the guest's hand has left the bell knob, he will be branded "Front" on his forehead and imprisoned for life.

The office clerk has been carefully selected to please everybody, and can lead in prayer, play draw poker, match worsted at the village store, shake for the drinks at any hour, day or night, play billiards, good waltzer and can dance the German, make a fourth at euchre, amuse children, repeat the Beecher trial from memory, is a good judge of horses, as a railway and steamboat reference is far superior to Appleton's or anybody else's guide, will flirt with any young lady and not mind being cut dead when "pa comes down." Don't mind being damned any more than a Connecticut river. Can room forty people in the best room in the house when the hotel is full, attend to the annunciator, and answer questions in Hebrew, Greek, Choctaw, Irish, or any other polite language, at the same moment without turning a hair.

Dogs allowed in any room in the house, including the w(h)ine-room. Gentlemen can drink, smoke, swear, chew, gamble, tell shady stories, stare at the new arrivals, and indulge in any other innocent amusements common to watering-places, in any part of the hotel. The proprietor will always be happy to hear that some other hotel is "the best house in the country." Special attention given to parties who can give information as to "how these things are done in 'Yewrup.'"

The proprietor will take it as a personal affront if any guest on leaving should fail to dispute the bill, tell him he is a swindler, the house a barn, the table wretched, the wines vile, and that he, the guest, "was never so imposed upon in his life, will never stop there again, and means to warn his friends."

T. J. FISHER.

WESTERN HOTEL ADVERTISING

(Ellison Collection, Lilly Library)

ished by white-painted notices praising "Gargling Oil," "Plantation Bitters," and "Salt Lake House, Salt Lake City, $1.50 to $2.00 pr. day." A British columnist reflected that nothing bothered him so much as looking for beautiful scenery and finding painted advertisements on every commanding peak.[13] In a land without barns, wood fences, or trees, there were no other objects on which to place an ad.

The job of the hotel touter or runner was to sell his house to arrivals at docks and depots, and sometimes to stage passengers on their way into town. The competent touter had a booming voice, strength enough to beat up any other touter, and the facility of fluent exaggeration. He could draw inviting word pictures of excellent service, low prices, comfortable beds, good food and, at the same time, belittle a rival house.

When a middle-aged Englishman arrived at the Seattle dock, he was amused by noisy touters. One called, "The Hotel St. Charles is the only first-class hotel in Seattle." Another topped him with "There is *no* first-class hotel in Seattle, but the Occidental is the only near approach to one." In Portland, when the best hotel had been flooded by the Willamette River, one enterprising runner sang out "My house not submerged," and got the business. Arriving in Leadville at midnight, Mrs. F. D. Bridges, on a three-year world tour, heard the cry "If any man says the Clarendon ain't a first-class house, I'll put a bullet through him."[14]

If a passenger hesitated, often a runner grabbed his bags and dumped them into an overcrowded hotel bus. British novelist Lady Duffus Hardy and her traveling companions met a large determined touter at Colorado Springs who asked if they were strangers. Answering affirmatively, they were pushed into the omnibus of the National Hotel. Her daughter, Iza Hardy, considered howling touters bad enough in San Francisco, but in Denver's Union Depot they pounced upon her party "like wild animals on their helpless prey." One shouted "Red Lion," and pulled them to the left. Another, working for the Lindell, dragged them to the right. A third yelled "Gilpin." And a fourth tried to snatch their baggage. Above the babel of voices they were relieved to hear "Grand Central," and thankfully departed in that carriage for their reserved rooms.[15] Drawn by two horses, hotel buses were painted bright colors, with the name of the hotel prominently placed. They could be rented by the month, but the larger hotels furnished their own.

In 1879 a group of unsuspecting travelers just off the Oakland ferry was surrounded by seventy-five overeager San Francisco touters. Two grabbed one man and two others took his luggage, each heading in a different direction. Clothes were torn, bags smashed, pockets were picked, and above it all was heard, "They don't have anything but rotten fish to eat at that house," and "They have lousy beds at that house." In the same city another tourist, who arrived by steamer, was upset by touters who boarded "like pirates," and gave himself over to the first one that approached. The safest, quickest, and easiest way to reach a hotel was to know the name of a respectable house before arriving in town, go to its bus, and expeditiously get into it. But in any event, one experienced excursionist commended, "persons should securely fasten their luggage to them with ropes."[16]

Inexperienced travelers often had their baggage damaged,

lost, or stolen, especially in crowded railroad depots. However, an efficient Australian had no difficulty with his luggage. Arriving at San Francisco, he sent some of his trunks
ahead to New York City and received a check for each bag
he took with him. On approaching a town where he wished
to stop, he would give the conductor his checks as well as
the name of his hotel. Entering the hotel empty-handed, he
would give the room clerk the baggage receipt and, within
a half hour, the bags were in his room.[17]

After the boisterous encounter with touters, visitors next
faced the room clerk ("heir apparent to the universe"). As
he assigned the rooms, the comfort of the guests depended
largely upon him. John Clampitt was cautioned that hotel
clerks "were pitiless, unmindful of the sufferings of others
and utterly remorseless in all their dealings with their fellow-
men." Supposedly, a clerk deemed it a good day if he could
cause a guest an inconvenience.[18]

The Oxford historian Edward A. Freeman declared, "No
one in the world teaches you your place so well as the American hotel-clerk," who dealt with guests as a czar or sultan
might treat his subjects. Even in the West's largest hotel, the
Palace of San Francisco, clerks were criticized. Kipling mentioned that when the Palace's apathetic clerk condescended
to tend to a guest's needs "he does so whistling or humming,
or picking his teeth, or pauses to converse with some one he
knows." All this, Kipling reflected, was to impress foreign
visitors with America's sacrosanct equality, but the famous
writer gathered from his neat dress, dignified manner, and
the size of his diamonds that the clerk must be the superior

ENCOUNTER WITH THE
ROOM CLERK, SOUTH-
ERN HOTEL, ST. LOUIS

(from Clampitt, *Echoes from the Rocky Mountains*)

of the two. On the other hand, George Sala remarked that the Palace's chief clerk, "Count" George H. Smith, who presumably never forgot a face or name, welcomed him as a brother and assigned him a suite of four rooms, fourteen windows, and seventeen doors.[19]

In an age where the size of a stickpin represented respectability, wealth, and position, hotel clerks were famous for their garish displays. Many guests were amazed by the poor taste Western clerks displayed in their show of shirt studs and lavish scarfpins. Actually, these items were borrowed from local jewelers, for whose merchandise the clerks were walking advertisements.

A hotel sign in Wyoming boasted of the services of a room

clerk who said prayers, played poker, made a fourth at euchre, entertained children, retold the Henry Ward Beecher
adultery trial, and flirted with young ladies. Also in that
house was a waiter who belonged to the Masons, Odd Fellows, and Knights of Pythias, and because of his discretion
was employed to deliver milk punches and hot toddies to ladies' rooms at night.[20]

The most frequently described hotel employee was the
waiter, who was often as busy shooing flies out of the dining
room as he was serving guests. In the larger houses a well-
dressed headwaiter was in charge. Often haughty and sol-
emn, he would take a guest on a seeming tour of the dining
room and, with a lordly air, deposit him at a table furthest
from the entrance. An English poet and social critic observed
that hotel waiters served customers in silence while eaves-
dropping on their conversations. James F. Muirhead, percep-
tive author of *Baedeker's Handbook of the United States,*
granted that waiters rivaled clerks in the brilliance of their
dress, but that did not make the sight of a waiter's thumb in
the soup more inviting. At St. Louis' Lindell the waiters were
observed cleaning dishes and knives on their aprons and re-
placing them on the tables as if washed.[21] And at a Manitou,
Colorado, hotel waiters so recklessly flung dishes and plates
that one guest was not sure whether the dishes were directed
at her head or her table.

Not all waiters' serving methods were censurable. In the
better houses there was one waiter for every six customers.
Leadville bragged about its distinguished waiters; a former
member of the New Jersey legislature served food at the

Grand, and diners at the Clarendon were waited on by an ex-lawyer and a former Confederate general. A Central City hotel waiter apologized in the mining vernacular to a hungry guest that the "pies played out."

Although the white waiter predominated in the West, Negroes were not uncommon. Richard Tangye, an English engineer, declared that most of the Negro waiters at the Palace were adept at their jobs, quick and agile, and seemed to anticipate every request. A British world traveler found that Negro waiters were unequaled—standing behind his chair, they foresaw every wish promptly but silently and were observant without being bustling or pompous. The fault-finding Kipling, however, complained that the Negro waiter perpetrated in one meal "every *bétise* that a scullion fresh from the plough-tail is capable of."[22]

Due to outbreaks of anti-Chinese feeling such as the San Francisco "Sandlot Riots" in July, 1877, there was an unwritten rule in San Francisco hotels against hiring Chinese except for the laundry. Helena, however, observed no such code, for a traveler noticed that only Chinese employees were found in its hotels. Some proprietors could hire Chinese only after promising to ship their bodies back to China if they died while in their employ. In Nevada, Sara Lippincott found the Chinese to be very able waiters; they were not haughty and they minded their own business. Even with six of them about, one had a wonderful feeling of privacy.[23]

Chinese laundry methods were not so highly regarded. Richard Tangye described the unusual way in which they applied starch: taking a mouthful of it, "they blow it out on to the article in a continuous fine spray, while their hands are occupied in ironing." Their methods in the kitchen were even less pleasing. John Clampitt at a Nevada hotel became nauseated when he saw a Chinese cook make biscuits. While mixing the dough he squirted water from his mouth into a basin and, for the finishing touch, spat into it "his own Asiatic saliva sweetened by the moldering gums and decayed teeth born of opium joints."[24]

Many houses had foreigners on the staff to lend dignity and class. The cosmopolitan four-story Walker House in Salt Lake City employed a German barber, a Scandinavian bartender, a Dutch headwaiter, and an Italian porter. At a Yuma hostelry, an American novelist observed American, Irish, Chinese, Mexican, and Apache waiters, adding that one should not expect too much from Arizona waiters. He had heard of one who waited for any complaints from diners with one hand on his gun. At a Las Vegas, New Mexico, house an argument between a waiter and a guest ended with the fatal shooting of the guest.[25] Hotel employees, like landlords, were a touchy lot in the egalitarian West.

The hotel porter or "baggage-smasher" performed a variety of jobs around the hotel. He carried bags to the rooms (the bellboy at that time answered the room bells and transmitted guests' requests to the waiter, chambermaid, and porter), cleaned the lobby, and served as an alarm clock. In a California hotel one porter awoke the entire house looking for a particular guest. He pounded half-hourly on the door of a man named Brown who insisted that he was not going anywhere and did not wish to be disturbed. Later, the sheepish porter discovered that he had awakened the wrong Mr.

Brown.[26] Not trusting porters to call him in the morning, an eccentric guest at a Greeley, Colorado, hotel took a rooster to bed with him.

Drawing baths by pouring buckets of hot water into tubs was also part of a porter's job. In a land where many regarded baths as unhealthy, not all hotels had bathing facilities, or, if they did, charged extra, which caused Europeans to conclude that Americans were not extremely fond of bathing. Some travelers brought along their own India-rubber or tin tubs; others took baths in uncomfortable, crowded barber shops, saloons, or stables. Two English traveling companions staying at Denver's Charpiot's Hotel in 1876 were pleasantly surprised at finding good meals and bathtubs—the first since St. Louis. Twenty years earlier, St. Louis hotels had offered less than adequate bathing facilities. A woman traveler from Massachusetts arrived at one hotel and found the bath water the "color of dirty soap-suds"! When the mud settled and was less than a finger deep, she carefully poured off the cleaner water and took a bath.[27]

While taking a bath in a Yellowstone Park hotel, Mrs. Edward Carbutt became disquieted upon seeing a grasshopper come through the pipes. But she fared better than a woman in a Santa Barbara hotel who was unnerved when a tarantula plopped into her bath water. A bath in an Austin, Nevada, hotel was described as consisting of a couple of inches of cold water in a large tub, a bit of brown soap and a napkin. When a roomer at a six-room tavern in Muscatine, Iowa, asked the owner where he might wash, the reply was, "Wall, thar's the river, wash thar, and wipe on your handkerchief." The Reverend Lemuel Wells lodged in an Idaho hotel and, upon asking the proprietor where he could bathe, was told there was a tub at the top of the stairs. As he was stepping into it he slipped, and tub, water, and clergyman rolled down the steps.[28]

Most Europeans thought tipping was a distinctive American custom, but *Appleton's Hand-Book* for 1867 explained that in America, unlike Europe, it was not customary to tip at hotels, though it might be done for special individual service.[29] *Appleton's* notwithstanding, service did increase markedly if a guest tipped. One foreign visitor wrote that a misinformed acquaintance had told him it was not the custom to tip in America, but he discovered that Americans tipped

HOTEL MAIDS

(from Browne, *Adventures in the Apache Country*, Lilly Library)

106

more than Europeans. A frequent English visitor to the United States, Emily Faithfull, recorded that when she first arrived in 1873 she was reminded not to fee in hotels because employees would look down on the gratuity and regard it as an insult. But times had changed, this feminist mused, and within a decade antipathy toward gratuities had disappeared.[30] Even though some held that receiving a tip brought about a deterioration of character, the tip became as important and necessary an inducement in the United States as in Europe and, with a greater division of labor in America, the drain on a traveler's pocketbook was considerable.

Many foreigners believed that if one planned to remain a few days in an American hotel it was essential to give a dollar to the waiter at the first suitable opportunity, and to hint that there would be more to follow, provided the service was good. The trouble with this theory was that, in the larger houses, you would probably never have the same waiter twice. But a guest should be sure to tip the headwaiter to obtain the same seat at mealtime. In a Denver hotel Mary Blake discovered a waiter who refused her tip, but she would not give him away.[31]

There were no laws in the West concerning child labor, and ten- and twelve-year-old boys worked as bellboys and elevator operators. The elevator boy was probably the most abused and hardest worked employee. He was spurned by his fellow workers and labored long hours in a small, poorly ventilated cubicle, constantly jerked up and down. For performing these monotonous duties, he was seldom paid more than $15.00 a month.

The night watchman, on the other hand, walked the floors

listening and watching for gambling, blatant *affaires d'amour*, but most importantly fire, a hotel's greatest danger (in a four-month period in 1887 over fifty American hotels burned down). Some watchmen were more useful than others, for it was said of those in Texas that they carried guns and long knives and, upon hearing a strange noise, fired the gun, threw the knife, and rushed into the street yelling "police."

As more women went West, they became increasingly important in Western hotels, especially as maids and in the laundries. A constant complaint against maids was their knack for awakening guests early in the morning in order to make up the room, and then disappearing when a guest wanted a maid. At the better houses, maids changed sheets twice a week, and a new arrival would find clean sheets on his bed. The beautiful and brilliant Maria T. Longworth, a lady-in-waiting to the Empress Eugénie, despised maids who half-hourly expressed the wish to "get through your bed." Many entered without knocking, sat down, and examined books or whatever else the guest had. In some regions the maid turned out to be male. William Dixon complained that when he called for a maid "either Sam puts in his woolly head, or Chi Hi pops in his shaven crown." Female help could not be kept any length of time because "Molly runs away with a miner; Biddy gets married to a merchant."[32]

Waitresses were not much in evidence until Fred Harvey's system became known and copied. Perhaps it was for the best, for a waitress at the Dodge House, when asked if the hotel had any encyclopedias, replied, "Ain't seen none since we washed the beds in kerosene."[33]

[7]

Breakfast, Lunch,
and Dinner

EATING HABITS EVOLVED QUICKLY IN THE WEST. LESS THAN
forty years separated the cannibalistic, blood-drinking, and
intestine-devouring mountain men and San Francisco Palace
Hotel guests who dined on *Escalope de Veau, à la Guennoise,*
prepared by Delmonico-trained chef Jules Harder and su-
perbly served by white-coated Negro waiters.

In the early days Western food was highly seasoned but
monotonous and occasionally unsafe. On the Oregon and
California trails, foodstuffs of the overlanders consisted of
flour, beans, rice, hardtack, bacon or "sowbelly," salt, sugar,
dried fruit, and coffee. Most of the cooking was done in
Dutch ovens and, west of the wooded regions, *bois de vache,*
or buffalo chips, were used as fuel. It was a heavy, coarse
diet, but sufficiently filling for the trek. In certain areas buffalo, antelope, sage hen, rabbit, and deer were shot; greens,

109

nuts, and wild fruits were picked; and in the Rocky Mountains trout, mullet, and salmon were caught.[1]

Miners found little relief at mealtime after working for hours in a cold stream. Salt or pickled pork, flapjacks, bacon, beans, and coffee were staples of their unbalanced diet. These rheumatic men cursed the unappetizing fare and, because of the lack of fresh fruits and vegetables, often contracted scurvy.[2]

Ranch grub was made up of dried fruit, potatoes, syrup, coffee, and the four B's—sourdough biscuits, bacon (called by cowboys "overland trout"), beef, and beans. Molasses and onions were eaten as antiscorbutics. A favorite dish of the range was "son-of-a-gun stew," cooked with vegetables, potatoes, and all of the cow except the hide, horns, and "holler." Cowboy Teddy Blue reflected, "Do you know what was the first thing a cowpuncher ordered to eat when he got to town? Oysters and celery and eggs."[3]

Soldiers' provisions lacked variety and often the pork and beef were wormy, the beans and potatoes were moldy, and mice ran through the hardtack. Colonel Philippe Régis de Trobriand, an accurate observer of army life, wrote, "The principal food of the men is salt pork, salt fish; and so there is sickness."[4] By the 1870's, with the increased use of canned goods, the enlisted man was offered a more varied selection, especially in fruits and vegetables. If a soldier wished such delicacies as eggs, milk, butter, or canned oysters he could purchase them at a sutler's store or at the commissary.

Newcomers to the West did not feel the lack of adequate food as keenly as they missed the genteel dinner manners of the East. The restless Westerner did not have enough time to enjoy an extended meal, nor was his food good enough to linger over. A New York physician and social critic recorded that when Americans ate it was "but one undistinguishable flash of knife and fork." He noted that most of his countrymen rushed to meals "with a dispatch which seems to abolish time."[5] The India-born author, Phil Robinson, sent west by the New York *World* to write on the Mormons, described Western eating habits as[6]

Dab, dab, peck, peck, grunt, growl, snort! The spoon strikes in every now and then, and a quick sucking-up noise announces the disappearance of a mouthful of huckleberries on the top of a bit of bacon, or a spoonful of custard-pie on the heels of a radish. It is perfectly prodigious. It defies coherent description.

An elderly British travel writer, John J. Aubertin, was annoyed by impertinent hotel waiters who were constantly asking if he were "through." While the food was usually palatable, Aubertin became convinced that America's idea of dining was "to get through—not necessarily in a hurry, but without pause." On her trip to America in 1870, Maria Longworth observed that Americans quickly shoved "down the various viands indiscriminately, terminating their repast in about ten minutes, and saving themselves from immediate suffocation by copious draughts of iced water."[7]

Because spirits were not usually served with American meals, coffee and iced water were the only liquids on the table. Indeed, it was said that the chief American food was water. To many foreigners, the coldness of iced water as well as the quantity drunk could only mean disaster for American digestive tracts. The Americans were warned by foreigners

DINNERTIME

(from Browne, *Crusoe's Island*, Lilly Library)

that the drinking of iced liquids during meals was extremely "injurious to the digestive powers, and serves to paralyze the stomach." But it would have been fallacious to think that the absence of wine and beer during meals indicated that Americans were abstainers, for the drinking of cocktails between meals had become a fixed habit in the United States.

Often the best food in the West was the "free lunch"

served in bars. With his drink a customer could have soup, stew, cold and hot meals, and "multifarious relishes." For those who refrained from buying a drink before knifing into the feast, a quiet disdain was shown. Often a less inhibited bartender shoved a "freeloader" through the swinging doors. Restaurant food in the West was largely made up of starch and protein and was almost always fried. It was low in quality and high in dyspeptic disturbances. And a substantial item was the hard, heavy, greasy biscuit concocted of water, flour, corn meal, hog fat, and saleratus. Pie was another common dish. John W. Boddam-Whetham journeyed to San Francisco by train and found at Western eating stops beefsteaks, ham and eggs, mutton chops and, invariably, pies. After watching many pies being gulped down he fancied that the "number of victims to intemperance in pie-eating must be enormous."[8] One sufferer penned a touching poem on "Dried-Apple Pies."[9]

> I loathe! abhor! detest! despise!
> Abominate dried-apple pies;
> I like good bread, I like good meat,
> Or anything that's good to eat;
> But of all poor grub—beneath the skies
> The poorest is dried-apple pies.

Western hotel food was often "rather rough," according to George Sala, but equal to the food in most states and superior to Southern cooking. Emily Faithfull declared that, in the United States, "God sends the food, and the devil the cook." She discovered that many hotels were more concerned with quantity than quality. A Negro waiter strengthened this belief when he told her that Americans did not care what they ate if only they had a lot of food placed before them.[10]

To the foreigner, used to a leisurely meal, this mode of serving and ordering was annoying. Here, everything came on tiny oval plates. Some Europeans concluded that the method of ordering the complete meal as soon as one sat down was curious, and could only lead to the apple pudding arriving with the soup.

While most informed travelers in the West expected poor food, Samuel Bowles naively imagined that every village of 500 persons or more on the Pacific coast had restaurants with fine Italian and French cooks. But he soon discovered an exception where rancid bacon, archaic beans, and "villainous mustard" were offered. There, if a guest declined the first two items, he was generously directed by the owner to help himself to the mustard. Easterners built churches and schools before they built restaurants, but Westerners built restaurants first. Bowles put it concisely, if not delicately, "the seat of empire, in its travel westward, changes its base from soul to stomach, from brains to bowels."[11]

Many restaurants and hotels hired professional hunters to procure fresh meat such as buffalo, antelope, deer, and waterfowl. To the Western mind, the fresher the meat, the better. The German proprietor at a La Junta, Colorado, restaurant told inquisitive Emily Faithfull that Americans did not understand a thing about preserving meat; "they kill and cook right away."[12] "Off the hoof" meat was thought barbarous by the English, who linked eating habits, good food, and its correct preparation with the advanced cultures of England and France.

Although some British complained about the unaged

meat and others about the dangers of iced water, more were inconvenienced by dining hours (breakfast was usually served from 7 to 9 A.M., lunch 12 to 2 P.M. and dinner 6 to 8 P.M.). Many felt that there was no greater form of despotism than American hotel meal hours and "neither love nor money will obtain anything to eat save at those fixed periods." Arriving at Denver's Grand Central Hotel, Lady Duffus Hardy, tired and hungry after five days of traveling, asked for food but was told that nothing could be had until morning. A Negro porter finally consented to look for something, and returned a short time later with rancid butter sandwiches and a bottle of beer.[13] This regulated meal schedule was incompatible with the freedom-loving ways of the Westerner, but it appears that only Easterners and Europeans lodged complaints.

Baedeker's travel guide to America warned that no American hotel would be considered first-class, or receive the sought-after asterisk of commendation, if it refused to serve a guest who had missed the regular dining time, but evidently this denunciation had little effect. James Muirhead was convinced that even the most excellent dinner would be spoiled by the "Draconian regulation" that it be eaten only between certain hours. James Burnley disclosed a contrasting point of view in his belief that Western mealtimes had an "elasticity" which travelers would enjoy. And, with such a large selection of food at American hotels, Burnley wrote that a guest could "have 'plain living and high thinking,' or high living and indigestion, just as you choose so varied is the fare."[14]

Much the same could be said for railroad food. Before the advent of the dining car, it was the policy of railroads to schedule three stops a day for meals at dining stations. Sometimes these were at hotels, restaurants, or lunch counters affiliated with the railroads. A Prussian-born Western publicist, while working for the Southern Pacific Railroad, boasted that the food at many stops was well cooked and served "with actual elegance." And Boddam-Whetham found at a dining station in Evanston, Wyoming, clean surroundings and "better than usual" food. Other stops known for their good food were Cheyenne and Laramie. Mary Blake was pleased to find that train-stop food was agreeable, owing to the prevalence of the tin can; but this Eastern lady wrote, no doubt with levity, that she was tired of the same menu of chops, steaks, Saratoga chips, broiled kidneys, duck, green peas, and apple charlotte.[15]

The viands were more often poorly prepared, miserably cooked, fly-covered, and, for some, inedible. To Phil Robinson the food at "these Barmecide 'eating-houses' " was so dreadful that he quipped, "a horrible cannibalic outrage on the [railroad] cars will awaken the directors." Robinson predicted that if the cooking in the West did not improve, the country would slowly drift into barbarism. Albert Richardson decided that the repast at railroad eating houses had the "general flavor of dust and cinders."[16] Many travelers were advised to carry along a basket well-filled with crackers and cheese, boiled eggs, tins of meat, and anything else that would remain palatable during a trip, as in the days of stage travel.

At the larger train stops runners often came to the trains, yelling abuses at one another, ringing bells, and beating gongs to advertise their respective establishments. Passengers were allowed twenty to thirty minutes to eat a meal costing from fifty cents to one dollar. Often they left overheated cars and practically froze in the cold only to rush into overheated restaurants. Inside it was pandemonium; travelers were trying to grab and swallow as much food as possible in the allotted time. The diner who had a long reach, an alert eye, and a quick hand got his money's worth. An experienced traveler would attempt to place the platters before him and attack them singly or all at once. But often at these "swaller-an'-git-out troughs," just as a passenger started to chew, the whistle sounded and he had to dash back to the train. One handbook stated that most railroad restaurants were kept by despicable persons who served filthy food and were in league with conductors, who would not allow customers time to eat. A year of train travel in the United States would make a generous man selfish.[17]

A London criminal lawyer, stopping at several railroad restaurants in 1883, found the rooms poorly furnished with tablecloths of "doubtful hue," and waitresses or waiters ("they might have been either as far as their appearance went") dashing about pell-mell. Travelers were served amazing mixtures, called a "square meal," consisting of beans, potatoes, biscuits, and steaks heaped together on a single platter until everything tasted the same.[18]

At one train stop the host and hostess paid more attention to train passengers than to a group of hunters. One of the latter did not care for such cursory treatment. Banging his rifle on the floor he sprang up, hollering, "If ye don't bring my steak in two minutes I'll jump the house!" In an instant he was served, but the travelers never found out the meaning of his threat.[19]

With the appearance of the clean, airy dining car in the 1870's, Western food became more palatable, with excellent service by Negro waiters as well as menus reminiscent of Delmonico's. Green turtle soup, canvasback duck, English snipe, and broiled oysters were offered to the passengers at reasonable rates. Most travelers appreciated the good food, although some were upset by the sensation of eating in a swaying car.

Western railroads owned hundreds of eating places, but only one railroad, the Atchison, Topeka and Santa Fe, became renowned for its meals and for the man who ran the Santa Fe's restaurants—that "Western civilizer," Fred Harvey. The first Harvey lunchroom affiliated with the Santa Fe was opened in Topeka, Kansas, in 1876, when Harvey was forty-one years old.

Frederick Henry Harvey had come to America from England in 1851 with two pounds in his pocket. After washing dishes in a New York restaurant, he visited New Orleans; in 1855 he moved to St. Louis, where for a few years he ran a popular restaurant. In 1862 the energetic Harvey went to work for the Hannibal and St. Joseph Railroad as a mail clerk; later he was traveling freight agent for the Chicago, Burlington and Quincy Railroad. Through his exposure to railroad operations he increasingly felt the lack of good train lunch stands in the West and, in 1875, presented to the Burlington his idea of serving good food in clean buildings. When Burlington turned down his suggestion, Harvey made the same proposal to the Santa Fe, where he was given approval to go ahead.[20]

In his establishments Harvey insisted upon moderately

HARVEY LUNCHROOM AT MOJAVE, CALIFORNIA

(Santa Fe Railway)

HARVEY'S LA PASAÑA HOTEL, WINSLOW, ARIZONA

(Santa Fe Railway)

priced (fifty to seventy-five cents), well-prepared meals served in immaculate surroundings. Passengers were not hurried at his train stops as they had been at the earlier beaneries. The number of diners on the train was wired ahead, and a whistle blown a mile from the stop as a signal for the waitresses to put the first course on the table. Ample time was given to eating and few diners felt hurried or left hungry.

Harvey's arrangement with the railroad was to lease the buildings from the Santa Fe and equip the restaurants, while the railroad shipped free of charge the employees, furnishings, and food. By cutting his costs, Harvey was able to serve fine food inexpensively. Working in perfect harmony with Harvey, who had only a gentleman's agreement with the company for many years, the Santa Fe in a short time had the finest dining cars and stops in the nation.

Harvey opened fifteen hotels in Dodge City, Hutchinson, Las Animas, La Junta, and Trinidad, as well as in other towns. In 1882 when a Harvey House, the Castañeda, opened in Las Vegas, New Mexico, a few cowboys playfully rode their horses into the lobby and demanded drinks. When they began shooting, Harvey appeared and, with great dignity, ordered them to leave. Apparently impressed with his firmness, they did so.[21]

Formerly hotels had relied primarily upon room revenues and liquor sales, but Harvey led the way to increased food profits by offering customers excellent food, artfully prepared and courteously served. His standards were high; he conducted personal inspections, hired only the ablest assistants, and purchased the best meat directly from stockyards in Kansas City and Omaha. Although at one Harvey restaurant a cowboy, shocked by a rare steak, declared, "I've seen many a critter be hurt worse than that and get well," nevertheless, "Meals by Fred Harvey" was a sufficient recommendation to travelers.

His waitresses were known as the Harvey girls and, next to the pioneer woman, the well-dressed Harvey girls "represented civilization's advance guard."[22] They were under the strict supervision of a matron and were required to be in their dormitories each evening by 10:00 P.M. Friday night dances and Wednesday prayer meetings were part of their well-regulated routine. The girls were between the ages of eighteen and thirty, attractive, of good character, and when hired they were asked to sign a contract stating that they would remain single for at least one year. Fortunately for many Western males, Harvey did not hold the girls to this pledge. The hours were good, as were the wages—$17.50 a month was the starting pay, plus tips, room, and board. One pleased customer composed a poem for these black-uniformed waitresses:[23]

> Harvey Houses, don't you savvy; clean across the
>   old Mohave,
> On the Santa Fe they've strung 'em like a string
>   of Indian beads,
> We all couldn't eat without 'em but the slickest
>   things about 'em,
> Is the Harvey skirts that hustle up the feeds.

To the astonishment of more than one rugged Westerner, Fred Harvey insisted that no coatless man would be served in his dining rooms. He might eat in the lunchroom without a coat or he could wear a black alpaca coat offered at the

HARVEY'S BISCONTE HOTEL, HUTCHINSON, KANSAS

(Santa Fe Railway)

HARVEY GIRLS AT THE SYRACUSE, KANSAS, SANTA FE STATION

(Santa Fe Railway)

restaurant door. But no coat, no food. Harvey's concern with pleasing his customers was shown when an employee came to him grumbling that a certain customer was crotchety and could not be satisfied. Harvey responded that perhaps the man was odd, but it was especially important that they please the cranks, for anyone could satisfy a gentleman.

Harvey's distinction lay in his demand for cleanliness, attention to detail, respect for patrons, method of operation, and hiring of able, efficient personnel. He gave customers what they wanted and made profits in the undertaking. Through his example, he has rightfully been credited with bringing good food to the West and for changing many Western hotels from places to stop to places to stay.

Western food underwent a natural evolution for various reasons. The extermination of wild life changed the meat habits of the region; Easterners and Europeans were demanding more sophisticated fare. Although fresh food was difficult to obtain, tin cans and refrigerator cars brought a greater variety of foodstuffs to the Western hotels. In the last analysis it was the Westerner who, tiring of his dismal diet, decided to enjoy good food and respectable service.

[8]

Hotel Life

THE HOTEL WAS BORN IN THE UNITED STATES EARLY IN the nineteenth century with the opening of the $300,000 Tremont House in Boston in 1829. Designed by the then foremost hotel architect, Isaiah Rogers, the Tremont, emphasizing service and comforts, led the way in many things. It was the first hotel in America to employ desk clerks and bellmen, and the first to be equipped with water closets, locks on every door, soap and pitchers in all 170 rooms.

Distinctive for its largeness and use of contrivances, the American hotel was unlike the earlier small, self-service inns and taverns in size, comforts, and service. Anthony Trollope, the famous English novelist, remarked that Americans thought as much of hotels as they did of legislatures, courts, or literature; and "any falling off in them or improvement in accommodation given, would strike in the community as forcibly as a change in the constitution or an alteration in the franchise." A Frenchman, rambling through American

124

society in the 1880's, maintained that in Europe hotels were a means to an end, but in the United States they were the end. Hotels, he said, were to Americans what churches, monuments, and natural beauties were to the Europeans.[1]

Hotels were almost as important in the West as the railroads, and they frequently appeared together. Many houses sprang up at end-of-track railroad settlements and moved with the construction gangs. In fact, one hotel was moved so many times it was called the Wandering Hotel. A number, mainly near the tracks, were owned by certain roads. These railroad houses or "headquarters hotels" were unpretentious but usually comfortable, and served meals to rail passengers in large dining rooms. The El Capitan in Yosemite was built by the Central Pacific Railroad. Ogden, Utah, had two well-known railroad hotels, one owned by the Union Pacific Railroad and the other run by the Utah Northern. In Laramie, Wyoming, the Laramie Hotel, opened in 1868 by the Union Pacific, was managed by Philo and James Rumsey, who advertised the "Largest and Best Hotel on Line of Road Between Chicago and San Francisco." Following the Union Pacific tracks, the Pacific Hotel Company had eighteen hotels along the line in the 1880's. There were those who found these establishments unacceptable. Henry M. Stanley, the explorer-newsman, called railroad houses "literally whitewashed Mugby Junctions" (a fictional railroad station in Charles Dickens' *The Boy at Mugby*), built in the American architectural style of "long barn," and owned by men of "aldermanic rotundity" who attempted to cheat guests.[2]

Hotels, like railroads, helped to develop the population. Not only did they attract people into new areas, but to inhabitants of a region where "dead oxen are almost the only signs of life" they supplied a welcome change. Even a small hotel looked good to a cowboy, miner, settler, or traveler who had slept in a bedroll, wagon, or stage. In the West the better houses were popular because they offered a change of scene and a different tempo of life, and because they seemed to represent respectability.

Reflecting the manners and morals of American society, hotels were "a genuine production of the soil, . . . in perfect harmony with American wants and ideas."[3] Indeed, nothing mirrored the ideas, ways, and tastes of an area, or lack of them, as did the hotels of the West. They brought together persons whom the land had drawn apart; for the hotel was often the only place to eat, drink, and sleep, thus combining the services of restaurant, bar, and home. Hotels have been compared to Roman baths, for all that was needed to enjoy life could be found there. In its performance of these functions, the hotel became the most important social institution in the West.

In these hotels life was acted out—birth, marriage, and death. For a cowboy in a hostelry in Miles City, Montana, a victim of tuberculosis, a hotel was a convenient place to die. It was also handy for the vigilantes who hanged two outlaws in the dining room of a New Mexico house. A leading hotel magazine, commenting on the frequency of suicides in hotels, believed that they offered an "opportunity for dramatic effect." San Francisco houses were especially known for their suicidal guests. A man was found dead from strychnine at the Helvetia; another cut his throat at the What Cheer; and at the Nucleus a wife was murdered by her husband, who then shot himself.[4]

But the suicides in San Francisco were minor when compared with the methodical murder that took place in Kansas along the road from Fort Scott to Independence. In the spring of 1871 a recently-arrived family erected a store-tavern on that well-traveled highway. Bender was their name—mother, father, daughter, and son. A more bloodthirsty lot never settled in the West. They advertised that groceries, meals, and lodging could be found at their stand; and for over three years they robbed and murdered travelers. In all, nine bodies were discovered. It was never known if the Benders escaped or were themselves killed by a relative of one of their victims.[5]

Guests could feel safe in the larger towns, however, where the houses were usually well run and well kept, and offered most of the conveniences of home. And in fact hotels did become permanent homes for many Americans. James Bryce, the celebrated British writer and statesman, asserted that in America everyone lived in hotels "except recent immigrants, Chinese, and the very poorest native Americans."[6] Known as permanents, usually of the middle class, these residents found hotel life preferable to home life.

The reasons for hotel living were many, and a few Britishers had opinions on the subject. Boddam-Whetham surmised that family hotel living was prevalent because of the difficulties and expense of keeping house. And Charles Dilke judged that it was due not only to the cost and trouble of maintaining a home but to the absence of servants as well. The servant problem did cause many wealthy families to live in hotels. Even if a female servant could be found, she was often a churlish, inept wench who demanded too much money, nights out when she pleased, and gentlemen callers.

The shortage of women in the West put them at a premium, and many girls soon left their jobs to get married.

The frontier spirit of equality was especially troublesome to those who hired help, for Westerners scorned any type of servitude; consequently the servant positions were left to the Irish, Negroes, and Chinese. The Chinese, because they were usually tractable and faithful, were thought to be the best servants, even though some of them were opium addicts. Emily Faithfull maintained that in the United States "every man is as good as another, and a great deal better." A Colorado woman insisted that she never asked for a servant's character references, but the servant was welcome to ask for hers. And it was not uncommon for the lady of the house to call on a prospective servant. A San Francisco woman in one month had a turnover of eighteen servants.[7]

Samuel Bowles, noticing the absence of the hostesses at some dinners he attended in Colorado, was told that because of the lack of servants the women were busy in the kitchen and appeared only to bring in the dishes and pass the plates. That year, 1865, in Colorado the salary of the most ordinary female servant was two dollars per day with board. And by 1880 housemaids in California were making twice as much per week as maids in New York.[8]

There were other reasons why families lived in hotels: early marriages caught many women unprepared for the drudgeries of housekeeping; hotels offered a livelier life and more time for enjoyment and relaxation; and the belief existed that it was cheaper to board at a hotel than to keep a house. The trend toward urban living was highly significant, and no institution better represented the pace and freedom of urban life than the hotel.

Hotels provided excellent living conditions for many people. Iza Hardy found that family hotel living in San Francisco was "full of home-comfort—pleasant and bright as a perpetual picnic." She held that the stimulus of eating amidst two hundred persons in the hotel dining room would drive cares away. And if the weather was bad, it wasn't necessary to leave the hotel; in the lobby were books, magazines, and newspapers, and for exercise there were the lengthy halls. For those socially inclined, society was always present and one could meet interesting people. Another writer termed hotel living "co-operative housekeeping," for the residents enjoyed clean rooms, the services of a large number of employees, the opportunity to choose from an extensive menu, and the convenience of having all bills made into one. He favorably concluded that "Independence is the great charm of hotel-life."[9]

In spite of its advantages, not only foreigners but some Americans criticized hotel living. It was argued that most women who lived in hotels had nothing with which to occupy their time. In these palaces of pleasure there was little privacy and less opportunity to train for housekeeping. Charles Dilke thought that such a life made women unwomanly. Another traveler believed that younger women acquired an amazing coolness and haughty sophistication from living in hotels. Critics felt that a setting in which women had so little to do would naturally lead to immorality and scandal.[10] A place with so many beds could not be pure.

In Denver, William Dixon, on arriving at the Planter's House, spied a small sign on which was painted "Madame

Mortimer, Clairvoyant Physician." This woman advertised throughout the town that she could be consulted on "diseases of the heart." Dixon's room was next to hers and, since the transom between was open, he overheard her nightly business transactions. After a brief absence, Dixon returned to Denver and noticed that all of her ads were gone. Upon inquiring, he was told that she had retired to the "brevet rank of lady and wife." On the other hand, many women enjoyed hotels for the chance they had to show off their finery. The "hotel belle" or "rounder" with social, not monetary, motives went from one hotel to another, stayed long enough at each to wear all her dresses, and then moved on.[11]

Children, too, it was thought, would be adversely affected; besides getting unsuitable food and too much excitement, it was feared that they had too much liberty and would grow up too fast. After a year of observation, Emily Bates perceived that in those huge, crowded establishments any feeling of home life was impossible. Charles Dilke knew from experience that such an environment forced children to play in halls and on stairs, thus annoying guests; further, hotel surroundings made them forward—"ill-mannered and immoral." In his comments on Western males, Parson Brown concluded that poor hotels did much to create the outlaw. This early environmental determinist maintained that such horrid surroundings must naturally produce a spirit of recklessness.[12]

Hotels were America's great meeting-places, and often as many nonguests as guests were clustered about the lobbies and halls. To Europeans, American hotels seemed terribly overcrowded and noisy. Edward Freeman thought it strange that so many nonresidents used hotel writing paper, browsed through magazines in the hotel library, and reclined in the lobby chairs.[13] British visitors, used to smaller and quieter houses, criticized hotels in the United States for being too large, too overpowering. Population growth, America's love of bigness, and the spirit of competition prompted the building of larger hotels. In a dynamic age when some believed that anything worth doing should be done on a grand scale, there was a "perfect mania" for huge hotels. The early Western idea was that the best hotels were the biggest ones, and the Westerner was unhappy until he had both.

Another difference between the better European and American hotels was that American hotels featured "convenience of arrangement"; most things which guests needed were nearby. The American hotel was a community in microcosm. Conveniently located in the hotels were barber shops and clothes shops, as well as telegraph offices and railroad ticket agencies with racks holding a colorful array of railroad folders. In "tonsorial parlors" the price for shave, haircut, and shampoo was seventy cents, including "hair-brushing and the application of essences." While reading rooms and libraries were not as common as in Europe, there was usually a newsstand or bookstall nearby. Writing rooms, with pens and ink, were supplied with an unlimited amount of hotel stationery. Smoking rooms, customary in England, were not easy to find in the United States. Phil Robinson did not locate a "bona-fide smoking-room" until he reached the British-owned Windsor Hotel in Denver. In other hotels, when he had attempted to smoke, employees had asked him to move to a public hall.[14]

American hotels increasingly made use of annunciators,

ice-making machines, and bells to advance service, but this "gadgetry" sometimes caused confusion. A card placed in a Caldwell, Idaho, hotel room gave directions for the use of the annunciator: one push would bring the bellboy; two pushes iced water; and three pushes hot water. A woman guest not acquainted with this new service kept her finger on the bell, bringing the old German proprietor bounding up the stairs, visualizing his house in flames. He rushed into the room, and saw the lady standing with a glass under the annunciator, expecting water to gush forth. Grabbing her hand, he roared "Mein Gott in Himmel, vat you tink you do. De whole house go crazy mad mit dat bell."[15]

At the El Paso Hotel, Fort Worth, in 1878, Quanah Parker, chief of the Kwahadi Comanches, shared a room with another Indian, Yellow Bird. Before retiring, Yellow Bird blew out the gaslight, and, unaware that the gas had to be turned off as well, died of asphyxiation. Thereafter the chief had greater respect for white man's devices.[16]

An American once said, "Give me the luxuries of life and I will not ask for the necessities." Many visitors to American hotels concurred, but some felt overwhelmed by "all the discomforts that money can procure." James Muirhead found bells that would bring a cocktail to his room, but had difficulty locating bells that would bring him a bath.[17]

European and American houses differed in methods of billing. In the United States there were two types. The most common was the "American Plan," dating back to the 1700's, in which a fixed charge was made per day for board and room. With the "European Plan" there was a fixed charge for room only, with meals a la carte; this practice began in France and

132

was first used in the United States about 1840. After 1870 the European system became the more common, especially in the larger cities, where there were more restaurants; the American Plan was popular in resort hotels and the small communities and towns. In the latter part of the nineteenth century, charges under the American Plan amounted to four to five dollars a day; the European was two dollars a day and up.

An interesting feature of hotels was the guest register, provided by advertising agents. This was an important document not only for keeping an account of guests, but also as a very effective form of free advertising. Omaha's Herndon House register had a list of steamer departures, plus: "Use Seely's Catarrh Cure"; "Yankee Robinson Big Shows"; and "For sale 100 yoke of oxen and 26 wagons."[18]

Guests inscribed where they had been, where they were going, and what hotels they had visited. The register of Charles E. Peregoy's small, pleasant Mountain View House in northern California contains numerous comments, from sentimental poems to witty sayings. A visitor from Richmond, Indiana, penned, "Not Paregoric but Paregoy! A Name of Comfort and of joy! Here the tired Traveller racked with pains. A little of his strength regains." An exhausted traveler from London wrote, "My Joints is so tender. Such aches they injender the whole blessed day I am screeching."[19]

Maps of routes, drawings of scenery, and comments on the weather such as "Snow all disappeared from Premises," "Earthquake at 9 o'clock (light)," were jotted down in another California hotel register. And in November, 1868, the owner wrote, "Shut up Shop this Day for the Season."[20]

133

.

Registers were used for not only droll intentions. In the summer of 1874 four Kansas counties were to be organized for bond-voting purposes. The state law required that each county have at least 600 citizens before it could be established. None of the four had that many inhabitants, so the enumerators copied names from old hotel registers to make up the requisite number.[21]

As much a part of hotels as the hotel register was the bar. In this male domain, the bartender was king. At the better places he dressed well and wore diamonds and gold as frequently as the room clerk. He performed such amazing feats of liquid legerdemain that Boddam-Whetham asserted, "Such dexterity and sleight-of-hand is seldom seen off the conjuror's stage."[22]

The greatest of this special breed of men was the astonishing Jerry Thomas. Called "The Professor," Thomas could mix any drink—fizz, julep, cobbler, sour, sling, toddy, sangaree, collins, or cocktail. Thomas was born in New Haven, Connecticut, in 1825, and went to New York City in 1847; two years later he moved to San Francisco. After working a short time in the mines, he tended bar at the popular El Dorado and was made first assistant to the head bartender. Stout, sleek, and smiling, Thomas was the picture of the perfect mixologist; he sported a sparkling diamond in his shirt front, diamond studs and rings, a snow-white jacket, and an immaculate walrus mustache. No mere imitator, the inimitable Thomas was a creative artist, for he concocted the risky Blue Blazer ("The novice in mixing this beverage should be careful not to scald himself") and the ever-popular

Tom and Jerry. Story has it that the former was conceived when a huge miner in San Francisco demanded a drink that would shake him down to his "gizzard." For a time Thomas was head bartender at St. Louis's Planters' House and then at New York's Metropolitan Hotel; after a year in Europe, he opened his own music hall in New York. In later years he wrote a bartender's guide and mixed drinks at the Occidental in San Francisco and in Virginia City, Nevada, making over $100 a week; by 1865 he was again back in New York opening a new bar.[23] A few hotels had their special drinks— Planter's Punch from the Planters' of St. Louis and, from the Grand of San Francisco, the stupefying "earthquake jig."

Most European travelers did not frequent Western bars, which usually displayed prints of scantily dressed demimondaines and almost always Cassily Adams' painting *Custer's Last Fight*. An exception was the Frenchman Mandat-Grancey, who stopped in a saloon at a Rapid City, South Dakota, hotel. Standing behind the bar was a shirt-sleeved bartender who had a large bowl full of ice with which he mixed drinks such as "gum ticklers," "eye-openers," and "corpse-revivers."

The majority of Westerners, however, asked for straight whiskey, which they poured themselves, being careful not to overpour and be thought a neophyte. Drinking glass after glass, they stood at the bar "without winking or uttering a word"; this shocked Europeans as much as Western eating habits. Often a newcomer to the West was urged to have a drink by someone in the saloon. Those who did not mind taking an offered glass were well acccepted, but it might be dangerous to decline a drink. The cowboy was known for being touchy if somebody, particularly a "dude," refused to drink with him. Reporting a case in which a Britisher was forced to drink at gunpoint, a Cheyenne newspaper sympathized with both sides: "the cowboy was wrong in forcing a man to drink. . . . But, on the other hand, snobbishness is not the proper thing in this country."[24]

[9]

The Last Phase

THE BARREN WEST OF THE 1840'S AND 1850'S COMPELLED settlers to give what they could to the first overlanders—a floor to sleep on and simple food. But the welcomes faded as the westward movement gained momentum, and to fill the increasing need public houses appeared. These businesses were seldom an improvement over Western hospitality, but they offered food, whiskey, and a place to sleep—for a price. Called taverns, road ranches, and hotels, they reveal the rude beginnings of the West.

In that coarse land, hotel facilities changed for the better as traders and travelers demanded comforts and conveniences from hotelmen who had the foresight to recognize that profits were to be had. By the 1880's Western hotel development reached the last phase, and tourists beheld gigantic, awe-inspiring urban hotels such as the Palace, Baldwin, and Windsor, and resort hotels like the Raymond, Del Coronado, and Del Monte. As if to make up for early transgressions, most

137

were too ornate and too large, imitations of Eastern models Hotel after hotel rose, each more imposing than the last. It one had two elevators and was six stories high, then the next must have three elevators and seven stories. Such a mania so relegated hotels to symbols that many ran in the red. But they were built on optimism to fulfill a dream—no matter how young, no matter how remote, the West would surpass the East, if not in culture and sophistication then certainly in the magnificence of its hotels.

Few American institutions have received such an abundance of both praise and criticism as did Western hotels. But without this criticism and praise, penned by travelers in numerous books, letters, and diaries, our knowledge of hotels in the West would be considerably limited. Europeans, and the British in particular, were freer with comment than American travelers. They declared that the resort hotels were a delight, unlike anything in Europe, with an easy mood that lent itself to fond reminiscences. Yet they felt that nothing could compare with the smaller, quieter, uncrowded European inns. Europeans overlooked the fact, however, that those inns catered to the few. American hotels were designed to serve the many and, new and untried, were hardly a match for the well-established hostels of Europe.

Not many hotels of the old West still stand. The Del Monte, Southern, International, and Grand Central were destroyed by fire; several were torn down; a number collapsed. Others, like Denver's Windsor, became flophouses and houses of ill repute. Some are now colleges. The Hotel de Paris is a museum. Ghost town hotels attract tourists with haunting reminders of gaiety and gold. A few remain, symbols of a vanished way of life: the Del Coronado; the Brown Palace of Denver; the Menger, next to the Alamo in San Antonio; the Excelsior House of Jefferson, Texas; the Driskill of Austin, built in 1886 by cattleman Jesse L. Driskill; and the Palace, which was destroyed by the 1906 earthquake and fire but rebuilt to become one of San Francisco's finest hotels.

These hotels endure as monuments to a colorful and yet significant era in American history. For the spirit of the West lived in its hotels, in the myriad feelings and aspirations of the Westerner. Those structures represented the true flavor of the land—the broad, exaggerated humor, the lingering pathos, and the amazing perseverance. The history of the West would be incomplete without the dimension given to it by the Western hotel.

NOTES

1. HOSPITALITY OF THE OLD WEST

1. Mary A. Holley, *Texas* (Lexington, Ky., 1836), 137-138; Andrew F. Muir (ed.), *Texas in 1837: An Anonymous, Contemporary Narrative* (Austin, Texas, 1958), 60-61; Viktor Bracht, *Texas in 1848*, trans. Charles F. Schmidt (San Antonio, 1931), 67; Charles Goodnight, et al., *Pioneer Days in the Southwest from 1850 to 1879* (Guthrie, Okla., 1909), 145.

2. John Bidwell, *Echoes of the Past* (New York, 1962), 83-84; Walter Colton, *Three Years in California* (New York, 1851), 223.

3. Nellie Van de Grift Sanchez, *Spanish Arcadia* (Los Angeles, 1929), 351.

4. Chauncey L. Canfield (ed.), *The Diary of a Forty-Niner* (Boston, 1920), 124; Charles L. Brace, *The New West: Or, California in 1867-1868* (New York, 1869), 229.

5. Edward C. Abbott (Teddy Blue) and Helena H. Smith, *We Pointed Them North: Recollections of a Cowpuncher* (Norman, Okla., 1955), 126; Oliver Nelson, *The Cowman's Southwest*, Angie Debo, ed. (Glendale, Calif., 1953), 67.

6. Andy Adams, *The Log of a Cowboy* (New York, n.d.), 150.

7. Arthur P. Vivian, *Wanderings in the Western Land* (London, 1879), 260; William A. Baillie-Grohman, *Camps in the Rockies* (New York, 1882), 364.

8. George A. Forsyth, *The Story of the Soldier* (New York,

1900), 109; Howard B. Lott (ed.), "Diary of Major Wise, An Englishman, Recites Details of Hunting Trip in Powder River Country in 1880," *Annals of Wyoming,* XII (April, 1940), 116; John S. Campion, *On the Frontier* (London, 1878), 67.

9. Vivian, *Western Land,* vi; Edmond Mandat-Grancey, *Cow-Boys and Colonels,* trans. William Conn (Philadelphia, 1963), 36-37.

10. Charles M. Clark, *A Trip to Pike's Peak and Notes by the Way,* Robert Greenwood, ed. (San Jose, Calif., 1958), 11, 37; James K. P. Miller, *The Road to Virginia City,* Andrew F. Rolle, ed. (Norman, Okla., 1960), 14.

11. James F. Meline, *Two Thousand Miles on Horseback, Santa Fé and Back* (New York, 1867), 19; Richard F. Burton, *The City of the Saints* (New York, 1862), 53. Although later some road ranches became cattle ranches, they were not at this time synonymous.

12. Edgar B. Bronson, *Reminiscences of a Ranchman* (Lincoln, Neb., 1962), 310; Everett Dick, *Vanguards of the Frontier* (New York, 1941), 334.

13. Eugene F. Ware, *The Indian War of 1864* (Lincoln, Neb., 1960), 51-52; Maurice O'Connor Morris, *Rambles in the Rocky Mountains* (London, 1864), 48.

14. Ware, *Indian War,* 53, 52.

15. Clark, *Pike's Peak,* 41, 45; Fitz Hugh Ludlow, *The Heart of the Continent* (New York, 1871), 15.

16. Robert M. Peck, "Recollections of Early Times in Kansas Territory," *Transactions* of the Kansas State Historical Society, VIII (1903-1904), 489; Charles E. Young, *Dangers of the Trail in 1865* (Geneva, N.Y., 1912), 45.

17. Margaret I. Carrington, *Ab-Sa-Ra-Ka, Land of Massacre* (Philadelphia, 1878), 120.

18. Meline, *Two Thousand Miles,* 27-28; Carrington, *Ab-Sa-Ra-Ka,* 62.

19. Clark, *Pike's Peak,* 41-42.

20. Carrington, *Ab-Sa-Ra-Ka,* 57; Emily B. O'Brien, "Army Life at Fort Sedgwick, Colorado," *Colorado Magazine,* VI (September, 1929), 174.

21. Maurice Frink, W. Turrentine Jackson, and Agnes Wright

Spring, *When Grass Was King* (Boulder, Colo., 1956), 346; E. Douglas Branch, *The Hunting of the Buffalo* (Lincoln, Neb., 1962), 124-125.

22. Meline, *Two Thousand Miles,* 20-21.

23. Mrs. Orsemus B. Boyd, *Cavalry Life in Tent and Field* (New York, 1894), 46, 145; Martha Summerhayes, *Vanished Arizona: Recollections of My Army Life* (Philadelphia, 1963), 102-103.

24. Alexander K. McClure, *Three Thousand Miles Through the Rocky Mountains* (Philadelphia, 1869), 116; Albert B. Sanford (ed.), "Life at Camp Weld and Fort Lyon in 1861-62," *Colorado Magazine,* VII (July, 1930), 134; Burton, *City of the Saints,* 469.

25. Samuel L. Clemens (Mark Twain), *Roughing It* (New York, 1962), 45; Louis L. Simonin, "Colorado in 1867, As Seen by a Frenchman," trans. Wilson O. Clough, *Colorado Magazine,* XIV (March, 1937), 61.

26. Frank A. Root and William E. Connelley, *The Overland Stage to California* (Columbus, Ohio, 1950), 95-96; William H. Rideing, *A-Saddle in the Wild West* (New York, 1879), 163; William H. Dixon, *New America* (2 vols., London, 1867), I, 148.

2. EARLY WESTERN HOTELS

1. Matilda C. Houstoun, *Texas and the Gulf of Mexico* (Philadelphia, 1845), 223.

2. Joseph O. Dyer, "History of Galveston," MS, Rosenberg Library, Galveston, Texas; *Telegraph and Texas Register* (Houston), January 29, 1845.

3. Francis C. Sheridan, *Galveston Island,* Willis W. Pratt, ed. (Austin, 1954), 39-42.

4. Andrew F. Muir, "In Defense of Mrs. Mann," in *Mexican Border Ballads,* Mody C. Boatright, ed. (Austin, 1946), 116; Marquis James, *The Raven: A Biography of Sam Houston* (Indianapolis, 1929), 328-329.

5. *Telegraph and Texas Register* (Houston), July 8, 1853; Houstoun, *Texas,* 223.

6. Ibid., 224.

7. *Telegraph and Texas Register* (Houston), February 18, 1854; Frederick Law Olmsted, *A Journey Through Texas* (New York, 1857), 112, 107.

8. Joseph W. Schmitz, *Texas Statecraft, 1836-1845* (San Antonio, 1941), 158-161.

9. Inez S. Dalton, "The Menger Hotel: San Antonio's Civic and Social Center, 1859-1877," *West Texas Historical Association Year Book*, XXXII (October, 1956), 85-86; Harriet P. Spofford, "San Antonio De Bexar," *Harper's*, LV (November, 1877), 834.

10. Tom Lea, *The King Ranch* (2 vols., Boston, 1957), I, 345, 344.

11. William F. Switzler, "Missouri Old Settlers' Day Tales," *Missouri Historical Review*, II (July, 1908), 297-298.

12. Walter B. Stevens, "The Missouri Tavern," *Missouri Historical Review*, XV (January, 1921), 252.

13. William N. Chambers, *Old Bullion Benton* (Boston, 1956), 99-100.

14. Charles Dickens, *American Notes for General Circulation* (Boston, 1895), 253-254.

15. John T. Scharf, *History of Saint Louis* (2 vols., Philadelphia, 1883), II, 1446, 1448.

16. Shalor W. Eldridge, *Recollections of Early Days in Kansas* (Topeka, Kans., 1920), 52-53.

17. Ralph H. Cross, *The Early Inns of California, 1844-1869* (San Francisco, 1954), 40; John Henry Brown, *Early Days of San Francisco, California* (Oakland, Calif., 1949), 36, 83.

18. Sarah Royce, *A Frontier Lady: Recollections of the Gold Rush and Early California*, Ralph H. Gabriel, ed. (New Haven, Conn., 1932), 99-100.

19. Bayard Taylor, *Eldorado* (New York, 1882), 304.

20. Horace Bell, *Reminiscences of a Ranger* (Santa Barbara, Calif., 1927), 427; Brown, *Early Days*, 110.

21. Charles H. Webb, "A California Caravansary," *Harper's*, XXXIV (April, 1867), 604.

22. "The Museum at the What Cheer House," *Hutchings' Cali-*

fornia Magazine, V (November, 1860), 207-208; "Library of the What Cheer House," *Hutchings' California Magazine,* V (January, 1861), 294.

23. Bell, *Reminiscences,* 5-7.

24. Harris Newmark, *Sixty Years in Southern California, 1853-1913,* Maurice H. and Marco R. Newmark, eds. (3rd ed., Boston, 1930), 227-228.

25. Ibid., 245, 347-348.

3. MINING CAMP AND COW TOWN HOTELS

1. Louise A.K.S. Clappe, *California in 1851. The Letters of Dame Shirley* (2 vols., San Francisco, 1933), I, 27.

2. Ibid., 27-30.

3. J. Ross Browne, *Adventures in the Apache Country* (New York, 1869), 364-365.

4. J. Ross Browne, *Crusoe's Island* (New York, 1864), 378; Browne, *Adventures,* 367; John W. Clampitt, *Echoes from the Rocky Mountains* (Chicago, 1890), 597.

5. James K. P. Miller, *The Road to Virginia City,* Andrew F. Rolle, ed. (Norman, Okla., 1960), 75, 78.

6. Albert D. Richardson, *Beyond the Mississippi* (Hartford, Conn., 1867), 479.

7. Henry N. Maguire, *Historical Sketch and Essay on ... Montana* (Helena, 1868), 115, 117; Carrie A. Strahorn, *Fifteen Thousand Miles by Stage* (New York, 1911), 87.

8. H. Minar Shoebotham, *Anaconda: Life of Marcus Daly the Copper King* (Harrisburg, Pa., 1956), 104-106; Isaac F. Marcosson, *Anaconda* (New York, 1957), 54.

9. William D. Bickham, *From Ohio to the Rocky Mountains* (Dayton, Ohio, 1879), 151.

10. Elmer Ellis, *Henry Moore Teller, Defender of the West* (Caldwell, Idaho, 1941), 86; Writers' Program, *Colorado: A Guide to the Highest State* (New York, 1941), 266.

11. Ernest Ingersoll, "The Camp of the Carbonates, Ups and

Downs in Leadville," *Scribner's Monthly*, XVIII (October, 1879), 804-806.

12. Lewis A. Kent, *Leadville: The City* (Denver, 1880), 136; Lewis C. Gandy, *The Tabors: A Footnote of Western History* (New York, 1934), 211.

13. Ichabod S. Bartlett (ed.), *History of Wyoming* (3 vols., Chicago, 1918), I, 137.

14. Gene M. Gressley, "Hotel de Paris and Its Creator," *Colorado Magazine*, XXXII (January, 1955), 28-42.

15. Charles F. Lummis, *The Land of the Poco Tiempo* (New York, 1893), 17; Browne, *Adventures*, 133.

16. John G. Bourke, *On the Border with Crook* (Columbus, Ohio, 1950), 61-62.

17. Will C. Barnes, *Apaches and Longhorns*, Frank C. Lockwood, ed. (Los Angeles, 1941), 17-18; Andy Adams, *The Log of a Cowboy* (New York, n.d.), 87.

18. Joseph G. McCoy, *Historic Sketches of the Cattle Trade of the West and Southwest*, Ralph P. Bieber, ed. (Glendale, Calif., 1940), 116-117.

19. George Jelinek, *Ninety Years of Ellsworth* (Ellsworth, Kans., 1957), no pagination.

20. Wayne Gard, *The Chisholm Trail* (Norman, Okla., 1954), 185, 213.

21. Dodge City *Times*, June 8, 1878.

22. James D. Horan, *Across the Cimarron* (New York, 1956), 50.

23. Charles C. Lowther, *Dodge City, Kansas* (Philadelphia, 1940), 86-88.

24. Robert M. Wright, *Dodge City, the Cowboy Capital* (Wichita, Kans., 1913), 226-227.

4. SHACKS AND PALACES

1. Lemuel H. Wells, *A Pioneer Missionary* (Seattle, 1931), 92-93.

2. John Codman, *The Mormon Country* (New York, 1874), 20,

33-34; Lee Meriwether, *The Tramp at Home* (New York, 1889), 159, 163.

3. George W. Kennedy, *The Pioneer Campfire in Four Parts* (Portland, 1913), 237-238.

4. Nannie T. Alderson and Helena H. Smith, *A Bride Goes West* (New York, 1942), 22; Lansing B. Bloom (ed.), "Bourke on the Southwest," *New Mexico Historical Review,* XII (October, 1937), 345.

5. Foster B. Zincke, *Last Winter in the United States* (London, 1868), 215; Charles A. Messiter, *Sport and Adventure among the North American Indians* (London, 1890), 242, 257; Bloom, "Bourke," 342-343.

6. George D. Lyman, *Ralston's Ring* (New York, 1937), 23-29.

7. Andrew J. Ralston, "Biography of William Chapman Ralston," MS, H. H. Bancroft Collection, Bancroft Library, Berkeley, California.

8. Oscar Lewis and Carroll D. Hall, *Bonanza Inn* (New York, 1959), 32-35.

9. Joseph A. Baird, *Time's Wonderous Changes. San Francisco Architecture 1776-1915* (San Francisco, 1962), 27.

10. *Graphic News* (Chicago), September 24, 1887; "The Palace Hotel," *Overland Monthly,* XV (September, 1875), 299; Mary Goodrich, *The Palace Hotel* (San Francisco, 1930), 30.

11. Jefferson Williamson, *The American Hotel* (New York, 1930), 94.

12. Lewis and Hall, *Bonanza Inn,* 52; Benjamin F. Taylor, *Between the Gates* (Chicago, 1879), 71-72; Rudyard Kipling, *American Notes* (New York, n.d.), 25; *Hotel Mail,* V (March 13, 1880), 2.

13. Robert U. Johnson, *Remembered Yesterdays* (Boston, 1923), 279-280.

14. Eddie Foy and Alvin F. Harlow, *Clowning Through Life* (New York, 1928), 163.

15. *Souvenir of the Baldwin Hotel, San Francisco* (San Francisco, 1887?), no pagination; Carl B. Glasscock, *Lucky Baldwin* (New York, 1933), 192-193; Harold Kirker, *California's Architectural Frontier* (San Marino, Calif., 1960), 96.

16. James H. Bates, *Notes of a Tour in Mexico and California* (New York, 1887), 121.

17. Howard L. Conard, *"Uncle Dick" Wootton* (Columbus, Ohio, 1950), 384.

18. Horace Greeley, *An Overland Journey* (New York, 1860), 162; Henry Villard, *Memoirs of Henry Villard* (2 vols., Boston, 1904), I, 124.

19. Maurice O'Connor Morris, *Rambles in the Rocky Mountains* (London, 1864), 77; Charles W. Dilke, *Greater Britain* (New York, 1869), 92.

20. John W. Buchanan and Doris G. Buchanan, *A Story of the Fabulous Windsor Hotel* (Denver, 1956), 5-17.

21. Edward Money, *The Truth About America* (London, 1886), 136-137.

22. Zincke, *Last Winter*, 212-214; C. J. Worthington (ed.), *The Woman in Battle* (Richmond, Va., 1876), 578-579.

23. Richard F. Burton, *The City of the Saints* (New York, 1862), 201-202.

24. Ibid.

25. M. Le Baron de Hübner, *A Ramble Round the World, 1871*, trans. Lady Herbert (New York, 1875), 75, 81; William F. Rae, *Westward by Rail* (London, 1870), 104.

26. George A. Crofutt, *Crofutt's New Overland Tourist and Pacific Coast Guide* (Chicago, 1878), 126.

27. George A. Sala, *America Revisited* (2 vols., London, 1882), II, 159, 158.

28. George Francis Train, *My Life in Many States and in Foreign Lands* (New York, 1902), 294-296.

29. William M. Bell, *Other Countries* (2 vols., London, 1872), I, 284, 287.

5. RESORT HOTELS

1. Caroline H. Dall, *My First Holiday* (Boston, 1881), 333.

2. Robert Louis Stevenson, *Across the Plains* (New York, 1895), 107.

3. *Hotel Del Monte* (San Francisco, 1897), no pagination.

4. Ben C. Truman, *Monterey, California: The Most Charming Winter Resort in the World* (Monterey?, 1881?), 7-8.

5. Susie C. Clark, *The Round Trip* (Boston, 1890), 115-116, 118.

6. W. A. Swanberg, *Citizen Hearst* (New York, 1963), 50.

7. Mary E. Blake, *On the Wing* (Boston, 1883), 223, 225.

8. W. Raymond and I. A. Whitcomb, *Grand Tour Through the Sunny South, Mexico, and California* (Boston, 1887), 8-9.

9. Carey McWilliams, *Southern California Country* (New York, 1946), 144-145.

10. *The Raymond* (Boston, 1886?), no pagination; Clark, *Round Trip*, 31.

11. S. L. Welch (comp.), *Southern California Illustrated* (Los Angeles, 1887), 64.

12. Mrs. Edward H. Carbutt, *Five Months' Fine Weather in Canada, Western U.S., and Mexico* (London, 1889), 110; Coronado Beach Company, *Coronado Beach* (Oakland, Calif., 1890), 6, 8, 13.

13. Hotel del Coronado, *Coronado Beach* (Oakland, Calif., 1890), 25-26.

14. Charles Dudley Warner, "The Winter of Our Content," *Harper's*, LXXXII (December, 1890), 54; Clark, *Round Trip*, 57-58.

15. Miguel A. Otero, *My Life on the Frontier: 1864-1882* (New York, 1935), 260.

16. Emily Faithfull, *Three Visits to America* (Edinburgh, 1884), 256.

17. Milton W. Callen "The Montezuma Hot Springs Hotel," *Denver Brand Book*, XV (1960), 192-200; Letter from Alexander W. Doniphan, July 22, 1886, in Ellison Collection, Lilly Library, Bloomington, Indiana.

18. James Burnley, *Two Sides of the Atlantic* (Bradford, England, 1880), 35; Amanda M. Ellis, *The Colorado Springs Story* (Colorado Springs, Colo., 1954), 24-25.

19. Marie M. Augspurger, *Yellowstone National Park* (Middletown, Ohio, 1948), 135-136; Emily C. Bates, *A Year in the Great Republic* (2 vols., London, 1887), II, 193, 183.

20. Carl P. Russell, *One Hundred Years in Yosemite* (Berkeley, Calif., 1957), 93, 96.
21. John W. Boddam-Whetham, *Western Wanderings* (London, 1874), 123; Sara J. Lippincott, *New Life in New Lands* (New York, 1873), 330-331; James B. Thayer, *A Western Journey with Mr. Emerson* (Boston, 1884), 84.
22. Charles L. Brace, *The New West: Or, California in 1867-1868* (New York, 1869), 86; W. Henry Barneby, *Life and Labour in the Far, Far West* (London, 1884), 71.
23. Arthur P. Vivian, *Wanderings in the Western Land* (London, 1879), 377.

6. HOTELMEN AND EMPLOYEES

1. Mrs. Edward H. Carbutt, *Five Months' Fine Weather in Canada, Western U.S., and Mexico* (London, 1889), 7; Edmond Mandat-Grancey, *Cow-Boys and Colonels,* trans. William Conn (Philadelphia, 1963), 22.
2. John Brown, *Twenty-Five Years a Parson in the Wild West* (Fall River, Mass., 1896), 42-43.
3. Lee Meriwether, *The Tramp at Home* (New York, 1889), 101, 103.
4. Don L. Griswold and Jean H. Griswold, *The Carbonate Camp Called Leadville* (Denver, 1951), 111-112.
5. W. B. Seymore, "Pioneer Hotel Keepers of Puget Sound," *Washington Historical Quarterly,* VI (October, 1915), 239.
6. George T. Buffum, *Smith of Bear City and Other Frontier Sketches* (New York, 1906), 140-141.
7. George W. Featherstonhaugh, *Excursion Through the Slave States* (New York, 1844), 79; Everett Dick, *The Sod-House Frontier, 1854-1890* (Lincoln, Neb., 1954), 406.
8. *Hotel Mail,* IX (November 12, 1881), 5-6; Napoleon A. Jennings, *A Texas Ranger* (Austin, Texas, 1959), 5-6.
9. Samuel Bowles, *Across the Continent* (Springfield, Mass., 1865), 201.
10. Will C. Barnes, *Apaches and Longhorns,* Frank C. Lockwood,

ed. (Los Angeles, 1941), 137-139; J. Evetts Haley, *Jeff Milton, A Good Man with a Gun* (Norman, Okla., 1949), 36.

11. Thomas H. Tibbles, *Buckskin and Blanket Days* (New York, 1957), 227-228.

12. *Daily Arizonan* (Phoenix), April 6, 1889; *Arizona Enterprise* (Prescott), November 1, 1878; *Daily Independent* (Helena), June 5, 1874.

13. Walter G. Marshall, *Through America* (London, 1881), 139, 143; Samuel N. Townshend, *Colorado* (London, 1879), 26.

14. W. Henry Barneby, *Life and Labour in the Far, Far West* (London, 1884), 158; Mrs. F. D. Bridges, *Journal of a Lady's Travels Round the World* (London, 1883), 346, 406.

15. Lady Duffus Hardy, *Through Cities and Prairie Lands* (New York, 1881), 269-270; Iza Duffus Hardy, *Between Two Oceans* (London, 1884), 153, 245.

16. George W. Romspert, *The Western Echo* (Dayton, Ohio, 1881), 365-366; J. G. Player-Frowd, *Six Months in California* (London, 1872), 16-17.

17. Alfred Falk, *Trans-Pacific Sketches* (Melbourne, Australia, 1877), 33-34.

18. John W. Clampitt, *Echoes from the Rocky Mountains* (Chicago, 1890), 146.

19. Edward A. Freeman, *Some Impressions of the United States* (New York, 1883), 237-238; Rudyard Kipling, *American Notes* (New York, n.d.), 25; George A. Sala, *America Revisited* (2 vols., London, 1882), II, 186.

20. Colon South, *Out West* (London, 1884), 93.

21. Hamilton Aïde, "Social Aspects of American Life," *Nineteenth Century*, XXIX (June, 1891), 896; James F. Muirhead, *The Land of Contrasts* (London, 1900), 16; *Hotel Mail*, V (January 31, 1880), 3.

22. Richard Tangye, *Reminiscences of Travel in Australia, America, and Egypt* (London, 1884), 136-137; Arthur G. Guillemard, *Over Land and Sea* (London, 1875), 304; Kipling, *American Notes*, 61.

23. Carrie A. Strahorn, *Fifteen Thousand Miles by Stage* (New

York, 1911), 87; Sara J. Lippincott, *New Life in New Lands* (New York, 1873), 173.

24. Tangye, *Reminiscences,* 137; Clampitt, *Echoes,* 468-469.

25. William H. Bishop, *Old Mexico and Her Lost Provinces* (New York, 1883), 474; Miguel A. Otero, *My Life on the Frontier: 1864-1882* (New York, 1935), 194-195.

26. John W. Boddam-Whetham, *Western Wanderings* (London, 1874), 354.

27. John G. Hyde and Samuel N. Townshend, *Our Indian Summer in the Far West* (London, 1880), 39; Hannah A. Ropes, *Six Months in Kansas* (Boston, 1856), 24-25.

28. Carbutt, *Five Months' Fine Weather,* 40; Bruce E. Mahan, "Three Early Taverns," *Palimpsest,* III (August, 1922), 254; Lemuel H. Wells, *A Pioneer Missionary* (Seattle, 1931), 93.

29. Edward H. Hall (ed.), *Appleton's Hand-Book of American Travel* (New York, 1867), xii.

30. Frank W. Green, *Notes on New York, San Francisco, and Old Mexico* (Wakefield, England, 1886), 32; Emily Faithfull, *Three Visits to America* (Edinburgh, 1884), 206.

31. Mary E. Blake, *On the Wing* (Boston, 1883), 39.

32. Maria T. Longworth (Thérèse Yelverton), *Teresina in America* (2 vols., London, 1875), I, 287, 295; William H. Dixon, *New America* (2 vols., London, 1867), II 21.

33. Charles C. Lowther, *Dodge City, Kansas* (Philadelphia, 1940), 55.

7. BREAKFAST, LUNCH, AND DINNER

1. Kathryn Troxel, "Food of the Overland Emigrants," *Oregon Historical Quarterly,* LVI (March, 1955), 17-22.

2. Daniel B. Woods, *Sixteen Months at the Gold Diggings* (New York, 1852), 57.

3. Edward C. Abbott (Teddy Blue) and Helena H. Smith, *We Pointed Them North: Recollections of a Cowpuncher* (Norman, Okla., 1955), 219.

4. Philippe Régis de Trobriand, *Military Life in Dakota: The Journal of Philippe Régis de Trobriand*, Lucile M. Kane, ed. (St. Paul, 1951), 262.

5. Robert Tomes, "Before, At, and After Meals," *Harper's*, LII (April, 1876), 729.

6. Phil Robinson, *Sinners and Saints* (Boston, 1883), 267.

7. John J. Aubertin, *A Fight with Distances* (London, 1888), 66-67; Maria T. Longworth (Thérèse Yelverton), *Teresina in America* (2 vols., London, 1875), I, 284.

8. John W. Boddam-Whetham, *Western Wanderings* (London, 1874), 58.

9. Frank A. Root and William E. Connelley, *The Overland Stage to California* (Columbus, Ohio, 1950), 97.

10. George A. Sala, *America Revisited* (2 vols., London, 1882), II, 292; Emily Faithfull, *Three Visits to America* (Edinburgh, 1884), 49.

11. Samuel Bowles, *Across the Continent* (Springfield, Mass., 1865), 201-202.

12. Faithfull, *Three Visits*, 49.

13. Lady Duffus Hardy, *Through Cities and Prairie Lands* (New York, 1881), 261-262.

14. Karl Baedeker (ed.), *The United States* (London, 1893), XXVII; James F. Muirhead, *The Land of Contrasts* (London, 1900), 15-16; James Burnley, *Two Sides of the Atlantic* (Bradford, England, 1880), 28-29.

15. Charles Nordhoff, *California* (New York, 1873), 26; Boddam-Whetham, *Western Wanderings*, 69; Mary E. Blake, *On the Wing* (Boston, 1883), 29.

16. Robinson, *Sinners and Saints*, 53-54; Albert D. Richardson, *Garnered Sheaves* (Hartford, Conn., 1871), 391.

17. James Redpath and Richard J. Hinton, *Hand-Book to Kansas Territory and the Rocky Mountains' Gold Region* (New York, 1859), 29.

18. William Ballantine, *The Old World and the New* (London, 1884), 135.

19. Alfred George, *Holidays at Home and Abroad* (London, 1877), 54.

20. Harold L. Henderson, "Frederick Henry Harvey," M.A. thesis, University of Kansas City, 1941, 6-8.

21. Charles W. Hurd, "The Fred Harvey System," *Colorado Magazine*, XXVI (July, 1949), 180.

22. Ibid., 181.

23. James Marshall, *Santa Fe, the Railroad that Built an Empire* (New York, 1945), 101.

8. HOTEL LIFE

1. Anthony Trollope, *North America* (New York, 1951), 480; Max O'Rell and Jack Allyn, *Jonathan and His Continent* (New York, 1889), 295.

2. Henry M. Stanley, *My Early Travels and Adventures in America* (2 vols., New York, 1895), I, 146-147.

3. Foster B. Zincke, *Last Winter in the United States* (London, 1868), 287.

4. *Hotel Mail*, I (December 15, 1877), I; *Daily Morning Call* (San Francisco), January 6, 1876; February 4, 1876; October 8, 1875.

5. Edith C. Ross, "The Bloody Benders," *Collections* of the Kansas State Historical Society, XVII (1928), 464-479.

6. James Bryce, *The American Commonwealth* (2 vols., London, 1889), II, 681.

7. Emily Faithfull, *Three Visits to America* (Edinburg, 1884), 278; John W. Boddam-Whetham, *Western Wanderings* (London, 1874), 37; Charles W. Dilke, *Greater Britain* (New York, 1869), 182; Henry W. Lucy, *East by West: A Journey in the Recess* (2 vols., London, 1885), I, 140.

8. Samuel Bowles, *Across the Continent* (Springfield, Mass., 1865), 62; John S. Hittell, *The Commerce and Industries of the Pacific Coast* (San Francisco, 1882), 99.

9. Iza Duffus Hardy, *Between Two Oceans* (London, 1884), 179;

NOTES FOR PAGES 129 TO 136

William M. Laffan, "Caravansaries of San Francisco," *Overland Monthly*, V (August, 1870), 176, 181.

10. Dilke, *Greater Britain*, 182; John Leng, *America in 1876, Pencillings During a Tour in the Centennial Year* (Dundee, Scotland, 1877), 254.

11. William H. Dixon, *New America* (2 vols., London, 1867), I, 126, 129; "The Summer Hotels," *Nation*, XXXIX (September 11, 1884), 218.

12. Emily C. Bates, *A Year in the Great Republic* (2 vols., London, 1887), I, 58; Dilke, *Greater Britain*, 182-183; John Brown, *Twenty-Five Years a Parson in the Wild West* (Fall River, Mass., 1896), 44.

13. Edward A. Freeman, *Some Impressions of the United States* (New York, 1883), 238-239.

14. Phil Robinson, *Sinners and Saints* (Boston, 1883), 56-58.

15. Carrie A. Strahorn, *Fifteen Thousand Miles by Stage* (New York, 1911), 533.

16. Oliver Knight, *Fort Worth: Outpost on the Trinity* (Norman, Okla., 1953), 101-102.

17. James F. Muirhead, *The Land of Contrasts* (London, 1900), 15.

18. Donald B. Allan "Herndon House," MS, James T. Allan Collection, Nebraska State Historical Society, Lincoln, Nebraska.

19. Mountain View House, Mariposas County, California, "Register," 1870-1878, Bancroft Library, Berkeley, California.

20. Golden Anchor Hotel, Sierra County, California, "Register," July 1, 1861-September 28, 1870, Bancroft Library, Berkeley, California.

21. T. A. McNeal, "Southwestern Kansas," *Transactions* of the Kansas State Historical Society, VII (1902), 92.

22. Boddam-Whetham, *Western Wanderings*, 356.

23. Jerry Thomas, *The Bon Vivant's Companion . . . Or . . . How to Mix Drinks*, Herbert Asbury, ed. (New York, 1928), xxvii-xxxvii.

24. Edmond Mandat-Grancey, *Cow-Boys and Colonels*, trans. William Conn (Philadelphia, 1963), 71; Edward Marston, *Frank's Ranche* (London, 1886), 196.

INDEX

CPSIA information can be obtained
at www.ICGtesting.com
Printed in the USA
JSHW022142181120
9687JS00002B/140